Praise for the Dating Goddess

The *Adventures in Delicious Dating After 40* series of books is based on the blog Adventures in Delicious Dating After 40 at www.DatingGoddess.com. Here are comments from readers.

♥ "Adventures in Delicious Dating After 40 is a wonderful composite of both the mechanics of post-40 online dating and what the practice of honoring one's self actually looks like. How marvelous your writing is to read. I spent about 2 hours reading and was riveted the whole time." —Maggie Hanna

♥ "At last, a dating writer who addresses requirements. You are SO right on! I'm thrilled to have found you!" —Rachel Sarah, author, *Single Mom Seeking*

♥ "Powerfully heartfelt and honest writing. You are inspiring." —Kare Anderson, Emmy Award winning writer

"I just love your writing. It is very fresh and gives the reader something to think about." —Kelly Lantz, President & Manager, 55-Alive.com

"Dating Goddess, you are like a, a, a, well, a goddess to me. You've helped guide me successfully through my re-entry into the dating world after 14 years. I'm an eager student and fast study, and do get myself into situations that others don't know how to deal with — such as 3 dates in one day — so thankfully you are there! You're the greatest, thanks for all you do for us!" —Jae G.

"I find your point of view much more interesting than other dating writers. Thanks for always reminding me to enjoy dating life no matter what it throws at you." —Sandy

"I love Adventures in Delicious Dating After 40. I really do like your honest and authentic voice — it's refreshing." —Wendy S.

"Adventures in Delicious Dating After 40 is really fun to read. Thanks for sharing your thoughts and letting us divorced single women know that we are not alone. There's a lot here that I identify with, although I'm not as brave as you are about dating lots of guys. So far. Love your blog — the first blog I've ever read consistently." —Elizabeth

"Thanks for a wonderful blog. You're doing a great job of saying what's in my mind. There's rarely a day I miss when it comes to checking in on your wisdom." —Paulette Ensign

Dipping Your Toe

in the

Dating Pool

Dive in Without
Belly Flopping

by **Dating Goddess**™

Dipping Your Toe in the Dating Pool: Dive In Without Belly Flopping

Second Edition

Cover design by Dave Innis, www.innisanimation.com

Book design by JustYourType.biz

Printed in the United States of America.

ISBN   Print: 978-1-930039-32-2

         eBook: 978-1-930039-15-5

How to order:

The *Adventures in Delicious Daing After 40* books may be ordered directly from www.DatingGoddess.com.

Quantity discounts are also available. Visit us online for updates and additional articles.

The Adventures in Delicious Dating After 40 books are dedicated to my ex-husband since he unexpectedly released me to explore the untethered life of a single woman. I then had the freedom for the experiences, lessons and insights shared in these pages.

Books by Dating Goddess

- Date or Wait: Are You Ready for Mr. Great?

- Assessing Your Assets: Why You're A Great Catch

- In Search of King Charming: Who Do I Want to Share My Throne?

- Embracing Midlife Men: Insights Into Curious Behaviors

- Dipping Your Toe in the Dating Pool: Dive In Without Belly Flopping

- Winning at the Online Dating Game: Stack the Deck in Your Favor

- Check Him Out Before Going Out: Avoiding Dud Dates

- First-Rate First Dates: Increasing the Chances of a Second Date

- Real Deal or Faux Beau: Should You Keep Seeing Him?

- Multidating Responsibly: Play the Field Without Being A Player

- Moving On Gracefully: Break Up Without Heartache

- From Fear to Frolic: Get Naked Without Getting Embarrassed

- Ironing Out Dating Wrinkles: Work Through Challenges Without Getting Steamed

Contents

Introduction	xi
Who is the Dating Goddess?	xiii
Do you have the right datewear?	1
Do you feel PHAT on a date?	3
What is your attire telling your dates?	5
What do others see through your glasses?	9
Dating with integrity	13
"All I seem to attract are players"	15
Are you a power dater?	17
Building your rejection muscle	19
When "be yourself" is questionable advice	21
The "pound-dog" syndrome in dating	23
How are you "wearing" your dating choices?	25
"It feels so comfortable"	29
Do you put your dates through tests?	33
The dating hobby	35
Is it affection or obsession?	39
Faux beaus and practice dating	43
The flirt-talk continuum	45

Living an R&B song 49

Are you making bad decisions out of loneliness? 53

What's your definition of romance? 55

A primer for how to become more romantic 59

What dates are you inviting to influence you? 63

Being "in wonder" about your date's behavior 65

When do you feel most vulnerable in dating? 69

Beware the duplicity trap 73

Being in step with the dance of dating 77

Are you sending (or receiving) mixed messages? 81

Are you date sated —or hungry? 85

Be willing to retry activities you think you don't like 87

Do your friends birddog for you? 91

Host a singles mingle 93

Are you out of his league —or he yours? 95

Do you give your date grace? 97

The worst two words in dating 101

If you're in the public eye, be careful how you
behave in dating 103

Why listening is so seductive 107

Avoid frivolous talk on a date 109

Cruising at festivals 113

Mistaking nice for interest 115

Nice guys don't have to finish last 119

Men's fear: she's a poser 121

Biggest surprise with midlife dating 125

Why the "Golden Rule" melts down in dating 129

A sensitive stomach can help you date better 133

Getting your cute on 135

Musician hits sour note 139

Does he know how to close? 143

The tingle of possibility 147

The first post-divorce dance 149

The triple-emotional-whammy wedding 151

99 men on the wall 155

Where are the men like us? 159

10 Tips for Successful Dating Over 40 161

The experiment 167

Lucy, the football and dating 169

Managing expectations 173

The fix-up 175

Dry spells 177

Setting boundaries vs. playing games 179

How soon is too soon?   183

Deafening silence   185

"I don't know if my equipment still works!"   189

Two-step for one   193

Following a man's lead   195

When your net worth is bigger than his   199

The activity partner   201

Dipping into salsa   203

Feeling powerless in dating   205

The low-speed chase   207

Resources   209

Afterword   211

Acknowledgments   215

The Adventures in Delicious Dating After 40 series 217

x

Introduction

This book is designed for anyone who is interested in stories, advice, and lessons from the midlife dating front. If you are over 40 and haven't dated in a while — or even if you have — you'll learn ways to approach dating with zeal, optimism, and hope. Even if you've had more than your share of negative experiences, I'll share how to glean lessons from those adventures, rather than just declaring that "all men are jerks" or "men are just looking for sex."

While most of the perspective is from a woman to women, men's comments, experiences, and lessons have been integrated as appropriate.

This book began as daily entries into my blog, Adventures in Delicious Dating After 40, which has been featured in the *Wall Street Journal* as well as on radio and TV. I wrote about my epiphanies from my and my friends' dating life. The best postings were culled to make this and subsequent books.

This book focuses on getting started on your dating adventures. We cover what you need to know as you begin your journey.

This book consists of three types of perspectives:

Lessons: These are specific experiences I thought would be useful to you. A few lines from my experience illustrate the points.

Insights: These usually start with an experience I've encountered, then the insights that experience spawned. It is usually comprised of around half story and half insight.

Stories: These are examples of situations I've experienced — or was currently experiencing when I wrote that piece — that I thought would be entertaining. Or I thought the story would help you see what kind of things happen in the midlife dating world so you'd know what has happened to others.

Because these writings were real time, as they occured, they are often set in the present tense. But they are not chronological. So a reference to "my current beau" may now be many sweethearts ago. I hope this isn't confusing.

I'd love ot hear your stories and questions. Please email them to me at Goddess@DatingGoddess.com. They may make it into the blog or my next book!

Who is the Dating Goddess?

I am a middle-aged, white, professional woman. My husband of nearly 20 years left me in April 2003 when I was 47, 11 days shy of 48. After giving my heart time to heal from the surprise divorce sprung by the man I thought was my soulmate, I started dating 18 months later. Generally, I have had a great time meeting interesting men, some of whom became romantic beaus, some became treasured friends, and some I never heard from again.

> *I am not a well-preserved, gorgeous, marathon-running middle-aged women*

In the beginning, I had dates with single male colleagues, but I quickly found Internet dating was the way to explore the most "inventory" and qualify men who I thought might be a good match.

I am not one of those well-preserved, gorgeous,

marathon-running middle-aged women. I have been told I am attractive, but I am overweight and not a gym rat. So while I am active, I do not match the description 90% of men's profiles say they want: slender, athletic, toned, fit. I have some wrinkles — what one sweet suitor mistakenly called dimples. I have what Bridget Jones called "wobbly bits," as most non-surgically enhanced middle-aged women do. My genes — and a lifetime addiction to chocolate — have made their mark. Yet I've met and dated some wonderful men, so even if you're not a lingerie model, you can find guys who will think you're attractive, perhaps even hot!

In my professional life, I am a bestselling author of workplace effectiveness books, professional speaker and management consultant. I've appeared on Oprah, 60 Minutes, and National Public Radio and in the *Wall Street Journal* and *USA Today*.

This book is intended to not only be useful to others and cathartic for me, but is also the genesis of a new topic for fun, thought-provoking speeches. I'm calling myself a dating philosopher and giving date-a-vational speeches! Let me know if you know a group who would like an entertaining after-lunch speech on how lessons learned from dating have implications in business and personal relationships and well as life philosophies.

How did I come by the Dating Goddess moniker? After a few months of dating dozens of men — one week yielded 7 dates with 6 guys in 5 days — my friends dubbed me this name. I liked it, so it stuck.

I'm purposefully not sharing my picture as I don't want you to think either, "How did she get any dates at all?" or the opposite, "Of course she found it easy to get 112 men to ask her out." I am not hideous (usually) nor am I stunning (without professional hair, makeup and Photoshop!). Some men find me attractive, some don't.

I continue to search for my "one," but I have learned a lot along the way, and my single and not-single friends have loudly encouraged me to share my experiences and lessons in the hopes of helping others navigate the adventure of dating with more success. And to have a delicious time doing it!

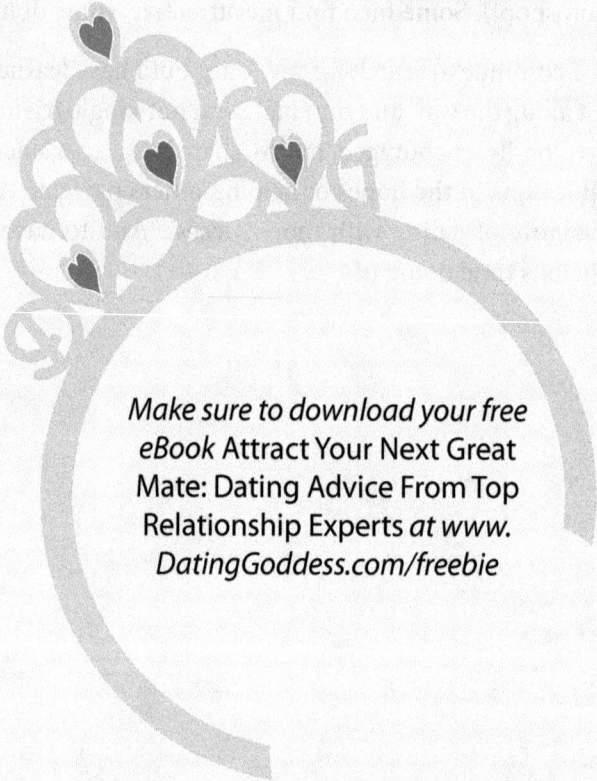

Make sure to download your free eBook Attract Your Next Great Mate: Dating Advice From Top Relationship Experts *at www. DatingGoddess.com/freebie*

Do you have the right datewear?

o you have the right datewear —clothes to wear on dates? I think it's especially important to have the right kind of attire for the first meeting. You know how important first impressions are — and how you dress says a lot about you.

Guys have shown up in wrinkled shirts and dirty jeans. Yuck! I don't expect him to wear an Armani suit on the first meeting — just on the second date. Just kidding. I do expect him to make some effort to look nice, just as I do. In fact, unless we are going to garage sales, the beach or hiking, I expect him to show that he cares about how he looks.

So what to wear? If you haven't dated in a while you may have to buy some datewear. This is tops, slacks or skirts that are somewhat casual, but are flattering and current. Your old jeans and t-shirt just won't do, unless you want to attract a man who wears old jeans and t-shirts too, or you have a killer body and look great in jeans and t-shirts. Most of us don't.

You don't want tops that are too tight or too revealing. I call cleavage-plunging tops "slutwear." You might show just a hint of cleavage, but don't go all Pamela Anderson unless you're a starlet. Your date will think you are loose, even though cleavage is now considered an accessory.

You may need to get new jewelry, belts and shoes if all you have is workwear and sweat clothes. If you have trouble pulling it all together, ask a stylish friend to help you, or make an appointment with a Macy's personal shopper. You really only need one or two outfits. You will be meeting a lot of guys for first dates, fewer for second, and even fewer for third dates.

Think about how you want to be perceived — approachable, confident, vulnerable, sexy. You only get one chance to cement that first image in his mind, so it's important to be strategic. I often wear a casual skirt on the first meeting, as I think it's more flattering on me than slacks. What do you look best in? Make sure it's clean, ironed and ready to knock him off his feet!

Do you feel PHAT on a date?

No, I'm not asking if you are fat, although many midlife women are concerned about extra pounds that have accumulated through childbirth, enjoying life, heredity, and slowing metabolism. I find it interesting that most of the overweight men I've gone out with don't consider themselves overweight, but near-normal-weight women often consider themselves fat.

> **PHAT:** curvaceous, voluptuous, women with a saucy attitude

I'm talking about PHAT: Pretty, Hot And Thick. This term has become popular with the under-30 crowd to describe curvaceous, voluptuous, Rubensesque, plump, plus-size women with a saucy attitude.

In dating, it can be sobering reading many men's profiles that say they only want a woman who is slender when you know you aren't. I am thrilled when I read that a man accepts — and sometimes prefers — a woman with some curves. What this says to me is that the man is a bit more open minded than many and understands there are amazing women in packages that are beyond size 2.

A movie titled "PHAT Girlz" starring Mo'Nique, focused on showing that women who wear queen-size hose can feel sexy and be attractive to hot men. Queen Latifah has never shied away from strutting her stuff in tight-fitting, revealing clothing. No longer is being larger a reason to feel one must hide behind matronly clothing.

Being PHAT is mostly about attitude. It is not being afraid to wear flattering, curve-accentuating clothing. It is about feeling sexy and allowing that attitude to come out. You exude self-esteem and like who you are. It shows through your walk, your posture, your solid eye contact, your easy smile, your flirting.

If you want some ideas on how to look fabulous if you are PHAT, rent Queen Latifah's "Last Holiday" (after her transition), "Bringing Down the House" and "Beauty Shop." Also, the aforementioned "PHAT Girlz."

If you have a larger figure, what do you do to feel PHAT? What do you do to show you feel hot on a date? What movies, actresses or recording artists do you look to for inspiration?

What is your attire telling your dates?

I s what you wear on the first few dates with a guy sending the messages you want? Do you find men relate to you differently than you'd like? It may not be them — it may be signals you're sending through your appearance.

When I began dating again I thought I had to wear what I saw on twenty-something gals: clothes that didn't leave a lot to the imagination — tight and revealing. Confiding my trepidation to a friend, she wisely said, "If you show cleavage down to your navel you'll only attract men who only want your body, not men who are interested in your mind or personality."

I took her advice and wore less-revealing, yet flattering and up-to-date clothes on first dates. I saved the plunging cleavage for dress-up events when I knew that my body wasn't the only thing a guy was after.

If you don't regularly wear sexy clothes other than on dates, you can forget the effect it can have on men you aren't romantically interested in. I was reminded, somewhat embarrassingly, at a dinner party the other night. I wore a top that was lower cut than I usually wear to a casual social event. I didn't think about it much until at dinner a male friend seated near me complimented my blouse. I offhandedly confided that it was a bit more revealing than I usually wore. The man seated next to him, who I didn't know, chimed in, "Why do you think we're all sitting at this end of the table?" I was suddenly aware that I'd been conversing with 5 unaccompanied married men seated around me.

"Why do you think we're all sitting at this end of the table?"

Silly me. I wouldn't wear that blouse on a first date, as I wouldn't want to give a man the impression I'm inviting more than getting to know him. I wasn't trolling for men's attention, and since I knew this party would be attended by partnered — not single — men, I didn't feel my attire would attract unintended focus. Dumb, I know.

Although some men claim not to notice what a woman is wearing, I'm sure they notice the effect her attire has on him. He may not be able to remember specifically the cut of your blouse, the style of your skirt, or how your earrings matched your necklace. But he does notice at some level if what you're wearing is flattering on you.

Recently, I chatted with a married friend about women's shoes and he said, "The truth is, men don't notice the shoes women wear." I knew he was a fan of Eva Longoria's Desperate Housewives character Gabrielle. I asked, "If Gabby wore baggy sweat pants with sneakers, flip flops or hiking boots would she still be as sexy to you?" He agreed that while Gabby could be sexy in a potato sack, her footwear did make her even more so. Her attire made a difference in her attractiveness to him.

In "Do you have the right datewear?" (page 1) I suggest you think through what impression you want to make on a first encounter. I think of dating clothes — dateware — like a costume. Just as actors have specific costumes to immediately broadcast many attributes like age, economic status, time period and personality, so does your dating costume. What you wear shouldn't project someone you're not, but should telegraph the characteristics you want your date to know about you: warm, friendly, stylish, smart, fun, or whatever you want to say.

What do others see through your glasses?

In Dorothy Parker's 1936 poem "News Item," she wrote of feeling that men were not likely to be drawn to — make a pass at — women who wore glasses. I don't know if that is still true, 70 years later. Some men, like a former beau, said he thought women in glasses were sexy. I think people can be appealing with specs, depending on the glasses.

However, with the explosion of LASIK and Americans' decades long love affair with contacts, I think fewer people wear glasses now. But I've noticed many of the men in online profiles are still bespectacled. Perhaps this is a function of midlife where more people need glasses.

What strikes me most, however, is how outdated those specs are. Many — in fact, I'd say nearly all — are the size and shape of what we wore in the '80s, some going back to the '70s. This means they haven't been updated in 20 or more years, maybe since the guy was in high school or college.

When I observe this, I can't help wonder what else hasn't been updated. Is he still wearing clothing from 10, 20 or 30 years ago? Is his haircut also from the Reagan era?

But, you may ask, what does it matter?

We all want to believe we will love and be loved for what's inside, not on the outside. But the outside often reflects what's on the inside. Does wearing outdated clothing signify outdated attitudes? Not necessarily. Does wearing hip attire show a more progressive perspective? Not always. Yet, many times there is a parallel. Even if your profession requires you to wear clothing that is the opposite of your point of view, you will often find ways to express your personality. If you are a liberal attorney who must wear conservative suits, you may express your perspective in avant-garde, yet tasteful, accessories. Or maybe you just consider your conservative attire as a costume for work, and let your quirky side show in your off-work duds.

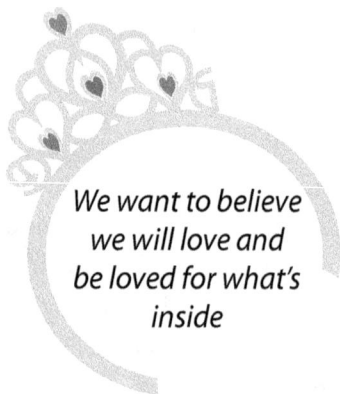

We want to believe we will love and be loved for what's inside

Glasses are one way to accessorize and express your personality. A male friend daily chose from his collection of 35 pairs of glasses before he got LASIK. He picked the pair that best reflected how he wanted others to perceive him that day. Another friend has a dozen pair, picking the one that matches her outfit. And a friend who speaks on future trends purposely wears glasses frames similar to those from the '50s, which are now considered hip.

Some people understand that glasses are not just a vision tool, but a way to telegraph something about them. They make a conscious decision about what they want that part of their "costume" for the day to say.

I'm a believer in getting periodic makeovers, as I think it's easy to fall into ruts and not see ourselves as other see us. Just as you would not wear a suit with gigantic shoulder pads or humongous lapels, as had been the fashion years ago, eyewear needs updating too. I think it is worth the investment to make sure one's glasses reflect the image we want to portray as well.

If you haven't changed frames in the last five years, it may be time for an eyewear makeover, even if you don't need a perscription change.

Dating with integrity

A friend shared how he's experienced that women he's beginning to date lie. We agreed that telling the truth, while uncomfortable at times, is really easier in the long term. Not only are you being respectful of the other person, but you date with integrity.

But what about white lies — little untruths that accomplish the goal, but are unlikely to hurt someone's feelings where the whole truth might? Like telling a guy who emails you that you've started seeing someone else, when really you're not attracted to him? To live 100% in integrity does not mean you have to tell him you're not attracted to him. It's easy to say, "We're not a match," before you start emailing or calling, but once you've begun that process and you learn you don't want to continue, it's hard to say the full truth.

> *Telling the truth is really easier in the long term.*

To me, living — and dating — with integrity means acting congruent with your values. If your values include honesty as well as kindness, compassion and consideration, how do you balance these?

You choose behaviors that cover both seemingly inconsistent values. So while some may get upset if the white lie is discovered, most will understand when you explain you wanted to be kind. Many men will say, "Why weren't you just honest?" To which you'll reply, "I was as honest as I felt comfortable being while still wanting to be kind, considerate, and sensitive to your feelings."

After all, dating with integrity can be uncomfortable. But it is ultimately easier as you can respect yourself for acting in alignment with your values.

"All I seem to attract are players"

I discreetly turned to see who made this statement and saw an average-looking, middleage woman at the table behind me at Starbucks talking to a gal pal about dating. She was wearing a low-cut camisole emphasizing three inches of cleavage and black bra straps showing underneath the spaghetti straps.

I made a snap assessment linking her comment and her cleavage.

It reminded me of a conversation I had with a gal pal when I was preparing for dating three years ago. I said I was going to invest in some low-cut tops to attract guys. My wise friend said, "If you show too much too soon, you'll only attract guys who are interested in your cleavage, not you" — in other words sex-obsessed players.

Somehow this concept escaped the fifty-ish woman behind me. She wondered why she only attracted players. Might it be that she looked like someone who was interested in attracting sexual offers? I think yes.

If I get attention in person from men I don't want to attract, I look at my "advertising" — my attire. Now, I realize some guys will hit on nearly any woman who wears a smile. But if I seem to get a rash of flirts and comments accompanied by leers, I think I've dressed a bit more provocatively than optimal.

Sporting lots of cleavage, bare midriffs and leg are the fashion now. I am by no means a prude, but I wonder if by wearing this kind of clothing women are sending signals to men they don't really want to attract. Not that we should wear always cover up with turtlenecks, long sleeves, and shapeless pants. Ugh!

Women argue that we ought to be able to wear whatever we want and be liked only for our personality. Yet the women who leave little to the imagination wonder why they mostly attract men who are sexually aggressive, and leave soon after a roll or two in the hay.

Have you noticed you attract a different kind of man if you show more skin than not?

Are you a power dater?

Another Internet dater shared that a guy she'd met online called and set a coffee date at 1:00 the following Monday. A little later, he called her again, apparently thinking she was a different woman, and set a 3:00 coffee date for the same day.

She was incensed. She told him off and canceled the date.

I didn't see why she was so angry. I've occasionally had two dates on the same day. So I asked her why she was upset.

She said he was a "power dater" and by having such close dates, it wouldn't let them get to know each other. He'd have to run to his second date (if he'd made it with another woman) after just an hour. She was insulted that he wasn't willing to give the 1:00 date with her more time.

Some dating books suggest that the first meeting be preplanned to last no more than an hour. The philosophy is that if you're having a great time, it will allow you both to reflect on the date afterward and look forward to the next one. If you let a first date go on too long, and you both like each other, a sort of honeymoon energy can develop where you only see the positives.

"What's wrong with that?" you ask.

I've had five-hour coffee dates. And I've experienced what the books discuss. I've become enamored with someone during that first date. While the feeling is exquisite to be in that state of bliss, in retrospect I see that I felt too close too fast. Things progressed too quickly that I should have allowed to take more time.

How would you feel if you knew your coffee date had another right after you? Would you be upset? Do you see anything wrong with scheduling two dates in the same day? How long do you think a first-meeting date should last?

Building your rejection muscle

One of the reasons people are hesitant to date is because of the potential for rejection. I would say you not only have the potential to be rejected — it is a certainty.

Let's look at this word "rejection." The dictionary says, "dismiss as inadequate, inappropriate, or not to one's taste." No one likes to feel dismissed, inadequate or inappropriate.

But what about "not to one's taste"? When someone says, "We're not a match" he is simply saying that you don't match what he's looking for. Is that bad? I don't think so. It saves you time and energy investing in someone who isn't a match for you, either.

I'm told that women have a harder time with rejection than men. My male friends tell me that while rejection is not fun for them, they have some muscle in this area that many women don't. As boys, men are socialized to ask girls to dance, request a date, go for a kiss. All of which risk rejection. More advances are rejected than accepted.

However, girls typically are not encouraged — at least not as much — to take these risks. I know this has changed dramatically over the last 40 years, but I'd say midlife women generally don't have as strong a muscle in the rejection department.

Because our muscle isn't as strong, most of us take rejection more personally than men. We allow it to affect our mood. We either begin to feel unworthy or man bash. Neither helps us on our path to find the love we want.

So what to do?

To build your rejection muscle put yourself in situations where you purposefully get rejected. I know you think this sounds crazy. But the more comfortable you get with rejection, the less it will affect you.

I once took a seminar where we were assigned to get 10 noes during our lunch break. We were told to ask people outrageous things, like "Would you take me to Paris this weekend?," "Would you buy me a new Porsche?," "Would you pay my mortgage," "Would you give me a back massage?," "Would you shine my shoes?" We learned that we would survive rejection. We were not being rejected, but our request was being rejected. (We also learned people said yes to things we thought were unreasonable!)

So email attractive men you think wouldn't be interested in you. Ask cute men you meet in the hardware store, Starbucks, or the grocery store if they would have coffee with you. If/when they reject you, think, "Thanks for helping me build my rejection muscle." And a few might say "yes."

When "be yourself" is questionable advice

Oft-heard advice to daters is, "Just be yourself." Well, what if "yourself" isn't very appealing? What if "being yourself" means showing up for a first date with disheveled hair, dirty, ripped clothes, and uncouth behavior? That's how you are at home, so isn't it truly being yourself?

On one hand, you shouldn't try to be something you're not. So if the above describes your usual self and you show up in an Armani suit and Prada shoes, you are not being yourself, unless you have, as many of us do, a wide range of clothing to choose from depending on the impression you want to make.

Within the span of who you are, strive to be the best you that you can be. So, unless you're looking for someone who loves dressing in comfy sweats, leave yours at home except if your early dates entail working out. And even if you don't usually wear make up, some foundation, lipstick and a little mascara isn't going to mislead someone into thinking you're a Vogue cover girl.

My model for the first few dates is to think of how you'd behave and dress if you were going to church/temple/synagogue. You'd put on clean, pressed, well-kept clothes, shined shoes, fix your hair and probably wear some makeup. You'd be well behaved and respectful. You'd smile and be friendly with others. Now, if you are going roller skating or biking on your date, you're not going to wear a churchgoing dress. But you'd want to appear your best in clean jeans or shorts and a top in good repair.

The other part of being your "best" self involves your behavior. Sometimes people ask why I don't more often call guys on their inconsiderate behavior. Part of it is I want to see what they do naturally without any intervention from me. Then I can decide what I want to comment on or not. The other part is if he is taking me out to dinner, I'm his guest. A guest does not nitpick her host. She is gracious and gives him some slack. If you were at someone's house for dinner, you wouldn't point out how often they interrupt, glance at the TV while you're in the room, or don't get in the back of the buffet line. You'd be pleasant, and then vow not to go back. The first few dates is too early to try to change someone's behavior.

So step back and look at what "be yourself" means to you, versus "be your best self." Be sure to don the latter for your early dates, and you can loosen up as you get to know and trust each other.

The "pound-dog" syndrome in dating

Have you noticed that dogs and cats adopted from shelters into good, loving homes are often very affectionate with their new owners? Many animals adopted from the pound have been neglected or abused. If they haven't been abused beyond repair, when they get around kind, loving folks they respond similarly.

I've seen this in humans as well. Often people become single after years of abuse or neglect from their exes. I've heard stories of people living in celibacy while married — sometimes for many years. Men have shared that their ex didn't touch, hug or kiss them for a long time.

I've heard stories of people living in celibacy while married

So when they are treated nicely and thoughtfully, if they haven't been psychologically damaged beyond repair, they often

23

respond with great affection. I've had men say to me, "You're so nice" when I was just being myself.

I've also had men misinterpret eye contact and smiling because they haven't received that from a woman in so long. And some can read an innocent hug or touch as if it means much more than intended.

Early on a man told me that I was so responsive to touch it was like a cat arching her back for more. I wasn't physically abused or neglected in my marriage. But I was neglected in a sense in that he said he didn't think about me if I wasn't in the room. So when a man shows he thinks about me when I'm not with him, I am drawn to him.

Have you been emotionally, psychologically or physically neglected in past relationships? If so, how does that show up now? Are you standoffish and aloof, or very responsive to kindness and affection? Have you dated someone who had been neglected? If so, how did you show your fondness without him interpreting more into your actions than you intended?

How are you "wearing" your dating choices?

I attended a sculpture showing of the master sculptor Jeff Tritel. Jeff and I went to college together and had lost touch 'til recently. I stumbled upon him and his beautiful work at an art festival, then was invited to a weekend showing.

Jeff gave me a tour of his recent work, explaining a few favorite pieces. I was mesmerized by his explanation of his art and his creative process. I wish I could have bought many of his pieces, as they are beautiful and the philosophies they symbolize are right up my alley.

Take "Field of Infinite Possibilities" — a man floats above a field of 3-dimensional shapes, while some similar shapes are imbedded in his body. Jeff says, "Our lives are built on the decisions we make. In this sculpture a man picks shapes from a field. He is constructed of similar kinds of shapes but as they are added to his body, they are changed by the interactions of his previous experiences."

Wow! Is that cool or what? A sculpture depicting the concept that our choices are embodied in us. I, of course, immediately related this to dating. ☺What dating choices do we "wear"? Nearly all of them, if they were more than a passing coffee date. Our choices shape our experience of life.

In fact, some of us wear our choices literally. Every time I am upset, frustrated or disappointed from some dating experience and choose a cookie over a banana, I wear that choice on my hips and thighs. Or when I'm angry at my current beau and don't express it appropriately, I can get a pain in my neck, exactly how I perceive my guy.

Some of us wear our choices literally

But there's more!

In Jeff's quest to make the piece an even more apt metaphor, he explains, "A removable steel pin allows the man to be placed in different position. The pin allows viewers to change their viewing experience by making their own decision on how the sculpture is to be displayed."

Wouldn't it be great if we could so easily choose our "viewing experience," e.g., perspective, and decide to see the situation from a completely different point of view, especially when the dating encounter has been less than positive? If you owned this sculpture perhaps it would be easier when you came home from a mediocre date to choose the sculpture's position, thus reminding yourself to change your perspective. Instead of thinking, "That was an hour of my life I'll never get back," it would invite you to say, "Let's see what I learned from that encounter."

To see Jeff's work, go to www.TritelStudios.com. Tell him the Dating Goddess sent you. Hopefully you'll find something in the catalog you can put in your home to remind you of some important concept.

"It feels so comfortable"

A gal pal described her relationship with her new beau with this common phrase. We interpret this as it feels right. If it weren't right, it wouldn't feel comfortable, right?

There are many reasons why being with him could feel comfortable. Perhaps he's easy going. Maybe he possesses characteristics you find appealing. Possibly he's got the same quick smile and sense of humor as your ex. Heck, maybe he even physically resembles your ex.

Or maybe he has some strong attributes that are similar to one of your parents or childhood care givers.

You know the old adage that women choose men who are like their fathers (and men choose mother surrogates). I've always rejected this theory because I have a toxic father and my ex was gentle, nurturing and non-combative. But after reading *Getting the Love You Want* by Harville Hendrix, Ph.D., I reexamined my ex's characteristics and saw more similarities than I'd cared to admit when we were married, although he wasn't toxic. Divorce helped me detach and see he was more like my father than I would have thought.

Hendrix, a marriage therapist, explains his observations from working with hundreds (thousands?) of couples. "[When looking for a mate, we're] looking for someone who has the predominant character traits of the people who raised us…. The ultimate reason you fell in love with your mate…is because your brain had your partner confused with your parents!"

Why would we choose someone with similar parental characteristics, especially if they were unpleasant ones? Hendrix says it's to work through childhood emotional and psychological wounds. Even if you grew up in a positive, safe, healthy, nurturing environment, "you still bear invisible scars from childhood." In other words, as adults, you are looking for a mate who can either emotionally comfort and nurture you, or will trigger some past hurts so you have an opportunity to deal with them now as an adult.

Why would we choose someone with similar parental characteristics?

My experience is that it takes a lot of awareness to deal with those triggers differently than you did as a child. Most of us immediately go into hurt and defensiveness unless we have the guidance of a counselor to walk us through the experience — which makes me wonder what part of our brain thinks we are innately

capable of dealing with the triggers a parent substitute provides.

Does all this mean it is a bad thing to feel comfortable with your beau? Not at all. My point is to examine the feeling of comfort before assuming it is a good thing. If you are used to being with an abusive person and the guy you're dating has those tendencies, it will feel comfortable. This is not good. So look closely at what it is that is comfortable for you and see if there are any parallels to past relationships. Then determine if these behaviors are in your current best interest or not.

Do you put your dates through tests?

Do you make men jump through some hoops when dating you? What do I mean?

Some women will only date a man who:

- makes the first contact.

- treats her to dinner at a nice restaurant within the first few dates.

- sends or brings her flowers within the first few dates.

- calls her once a day.

- showers her with compliments.

- changes his schedule to accommodate her.

- takes her on an expensive getaway.

- allows her to change his appearance or style.

The woman (AKA a diva) is insisting he play by her rules. She is not accommodating at all, but thinks she is such a prize that he must bow to her every demand. I have a few friends like this who are happily married so it must work in some cases. However, I think most men would be put off by such self-focused, demanding, spoiled behavior.

While I have some preferences, I don't have demands, other than that he behaves with integrity, consideration, confidence, communication and respect. Relationships involve compromise and you can't — and shouldn't — always get your way.

Do you have any tests you think are reasonable? One of mine is he must make contact periodically for me to know he's interested. I don't chase men. Once we've begun dating, I don't mind initiating an email or call. But I don't want to be the only one picking up the phone.

What are some of the tests for you?

The dating hobby

Have you found yourself feeling that dating is a hobby? And just like some hobbies, you do it more or less often than other things you enjoy. I find myself immersing myself in some hobbies, then totally abandoning them for long stretches. And just like the hobbies of belly dancing, scuba diving or parachute jumping, you need specialized attire — dateware!

In the first two years of my new single life, when friends would ask what was new, I'd respond enthusiastically, "I'm dating!" accompanied by a big smile. It was as if I was announcing my new hobby of scrapbooking, Greek dancing, or spelunking. My search for a new love had become a recreational avocation.

Is this a good thing or not? It depends on your perspective. If you are into sport dating, then you enjoy dating around and meeting a lot of people with no real intention of finding one for the long term. If you aren't upfront about wanting to date around, some daters resent this attitude as they feel you are wasting their time.

Others appreciate this more carefree attitude and gather activity partners like shoes, choosing which ones are best for a certain outing. (See "Men are like shoes," in the *Embracing Midlife Men: Insights Into Curious Behaviors* book.)

There are two downsides to hobby dating:

1. You may be commitment averse and not know it. If you've dated a lot and pull the plug after seeing a guy for a few months, it might be that it isn't just that you're too picky. Make sure you explore the possibility that you're afraid of commitment.

2. If you're not honest with the men you date that you're interested in only an occasional activity partner, he could be justifiably upset when he falls for you and you don't respond in kind. Unrequited is never fun.

Treating dating like a hobby allows you the freedom to meet people without the expectation of quickly finding The One. This also means you don't soon get discouraged. You are more able to enjoy the person in front of you and get to know him without pondering, "Would I marry him?" You are more relaxed, which means he's more relaxed, which means you can lighten up and have fun.

Be grateful that life is hard

However, you have to hold back from accepting an invitation from someone you

know you'd never consider a romantic partner, just to fill an evening. Unless you both have said you are just looking for friends and activity partners.

Just as with any hobby, be clear on the parts of it that you enjoy and stop doing it when it isn't fun anymore. No one likes to be around a lackadaisical or bitter companion for any hobby.

Is it affection or obsession?

Sometimes, early in the getting-to-know-you stage, one of both of you become so smitten that you find yourself emailing, calling, texting or IMing multiple times throughout the day. You can have an ongoing IM or text conversation throughout the whole day, getting little else done. Yet you are having fun, excited by the attention and getting to know the new person.

Whenever this has happened for me, it has been trouble. Yet when I've been smitten, I ignore the signs. However, if it is the man who is apparently smitten, I have learned to be receptive, but to create a little distance. How? By not responding as quickly as I might to an email, IM or text message.

Why?

Because if I'm not enthralled at the same level as he is, responding quickly and frequently can send a signal that I am equally enchanted. This is sending the wrong signal. Usually, at first, I am a bit cautious, having

learned it can be easy to become besotted with someone, even before you've met them. Then you've fallen
for the illusion of the person you barely know, rather
than the real thing.

*Be grateful that
life is hard*

Also, with just a
little encouragement,
some people can go
from feeling affection or
fondness toward you to
full on obsession. This
happened with a man
I'd met online. We en-
joyed each other's com-
munications, and it es-
calated quickly. The IM
responses quickened to where soon we were responding to the other before a message was fully typed. He'd
call me within 10 minutes of signing off the computer at
work, wanting to chat on his way home. He'd text, email
or IM me throughout the evening at home.

We met for lunch 4 days after our initial contact,
and he was already wanting to hold hands, put his arm
around me when walking, hug and kiss. Needy? I think
that would be an accurate statement. Even though I am
comfortable with and appreciate attention and affection, this felt like too much too soon to me.

The day after we met, we IMed a few times, then he
called a few minutes after logging off to talk to me while
he was doing errands. "I just wanted to let you know I
was thinking of you," he said. While I appreciated the

sweetness of the sentiment, I teased, "Thanks. I thought you might have forgotten all about me in the intervening 20 minutes since our last IM."

A few hours later, I received this email:

> *"I am writing this because I see myself falling back into patterns of behavior that I don't like. I am becoming obsessive about you, and I don't approve of that in myself. As you pointed out, I had spoken with you only a few minutes before, and yet I had to call. I have spent a number of years trying to work through this tendency, and I guess I haven't managed it yet.*
>
> *"You are a spectacular lady, and I truly want you to find someone who is as awesome as you are. But until I get my head squared away, that isn't me."*

I applaud his self-awareness to realize he was falling into old patterns. He had told me that one girlfriend had broken up with him because she felt smothered. I could see that. Obsession is never healthy. As we saw in "Fatal Attraction" and other works, it can lead to sad outcomes.

So no matter how much you enjoy affection and attention, if you feel you or he are obsessed, best to do what my guy did and back away.

(For the rest of this story, see "Yuck!" in the *First-Rate First Dates: Increasing the Chances of a Second Date* book.)

Faux beaus and practice dating

When beginning dating, I was advised to go out with nearly anyone who met my basic criteria, just to practice. Since I didn't want to take advantage of anyone, I kept these practice dates to coffee. These dates helped shore up my confidence and hone my skills at talking with men I just met about relationships and other topics that one doesn't usually bring up on first meetings.

I'm not proud to admit it, but I even had a faux beau. This was a gentleman who treated me well and liked my company, and I liked his mostly. But I knew it was not a long-term match. I called him my faux beau because he called me every day, we went out several times a week, and I was fond of

I knew it was not a long-term match

him yet I knew we were not a match.

When my conscience convinced me it was not fair to him to keep seeing him, as he would not find his true love while dating me, I let him know. He still wanted to see me, but I knew he wouldn't date anyone else if I acquiesced. I told him to date other people and we could do things together occasionally as friends, which we did.

So if you haven't dated a lot, consider practice dates, but be considerate. Plan for short-time, low-cost activities. Always be pleasant even though you know it isn't a match. And who knows, a practice date might turn into your soul mate!

The flirt-talk
continuum

I've noticed that flirt-talk typically starts out innocently — you share things you like about the other, compliment him, tell himyou think she's cute, sexy or a catch, comment that you're looking forward to talking/ seeing him again. In person this is coupled with smiles, laughter, perhaps light touches and other body language to show you like the other. It can progress — in one date or many — to hand holding, arm linking, hugs, kissing, and more.

However, I've noticed that more men than women don't seem to understand the subtle line between flirting (with perhaps suggestive innuendo) and downright explicit raunchiness. In fact, one guy ("Lessons from a bad date, in the *First-Rate First Dates: Increasing the Chances of a Second Date* book) began his "flirting" at raunchy.

Once one is comfortable flirting with the other, seeing a positive response, and feeling it is okay, you can move up the continuum. For many woman, however, this will take a bit of time and trust. In fact, some women (and some men) will never be comfortable either giving or receiving anything beyond initial flirting talk. I think it is critical to be conscious of the other's reaction and not press if s/he seems uncomfortable.

In fact, I've told men I "didn't want to go there" when they got too explicit for my comfort level, and they ignored me. They were the ones soon being ignored — by me.

And of course, neither party may want to go to the far end of the continuum. That's part of finding out who the other person is and where s/he is comfortable, as well as setting your own boundaries.

In the interest in helping define, then educate both genders, I thought I'd take a crack at describing a flirt-talk continuum.

Imagine a line where "innuendo" is on the far left and "vulger on the far right. The other words fall in between. Here are definitions to help distinguish the levels:

> *Innuendo:* an allusive or oblique remark or hint, typically a suggestive one
>
> *Suggestiveness:* making someone think of sex and sexual relationships
>
> *Titillating:* stimulating or exciting, especially in a sexual way
>
> *Raunchy:* earthy, vulgar, and often sexually explicit

Vulgar: making explicit and offensive reference to sex or bodily functions

What do you think about this continuum? Should there be finer gradations? In a different order? Other words?

And how do you decide whether or not to go to the next level? What if your date is going to another level faster than you'd prefer?

Make sure to download your free eBook Attract Your Next Great Mate: Dating Advice From Top Relationship Experts *at www. DatingGoddess.com/freebie*

Living an R&B

song

I love R&B music. It is romantic, sexy, vulnerable and has a danceable beat. So it is icing on the cake that Radio Guy, the newest guy in my life, is an R&B disc jockey. In addition to having a melodious voice, his words and actions reflect the R&B he's listened to five hours a day for 30 years. Did he have these sensibilities before and chose a job that reflected his perspective on life? Or did the music help shape his point of view?

In "How does music affect your dating?" (in the *Assessing Your Assets: Why You're A Great Catch* book) I pondered how our music druthers affect our love preferences. The male R&B singers seem to have no problem expressing their feelings — love, adoration, attraction, much more so than men I've met in real life. Is it because they are more poetic than regular guys, or is it just they know what sells?

Radio Guy has no problem expressing his feelings, even when they aren't macho. He's shared grief at a close aunt's recent passing, his compassion for her only surviving son's sorrow, his exhilaration at a new job offer, and — my favorite — his feelings toward me. He's able to share what's going on with him authentically, in a way that most men I've known less than a week would have difficulty.

So far, it feels like I'm living in an R&B song. He tells me what he likes and admires about me and how much he wants to have it work out with us. Luckily, he doesn't recite lyrics from songs as come on lines. He treats me tenderly in person and on the phone. It makes it easy for me to tell him what I like about him.

> *He treats me tenderly in person and on the phone*

In contrast, I dated a man who was so guarded I wondered why he continued to ask me out. On date five (four were low-key dinner and DVD dates), he made a comment about how he was "pursuing" me. I was taken aback, and said, "You're pursuing me?" I had no idea, since he wasn't affectionate verbally or physically. I thought he enjoyed my company so liked to hang out with me, but he never complimented me or made any wooing gestures.

Are you drawn to men who express their feelings? I find it compelling, as you don't have to guess where he stands. Granted, someone could lie and use well-rehearsed lines. But those guys are pretty easy to spot.

And who knows, if Radio Guy goes poof I may switch over to Country where the songs are a bit more about disappointments and love lost.

(For more on my rollar coaster with this man, see "Becoming a boo" in the *Ironing Out Dating Wrinkles: Work Through Challenges Without Getting Steamed* book, "Ninny-ness," "The faux vacation fling," and "Being played by a pathological liar" all in the *Real Deal or Faux Beau: Should You Keep Seeing Him?* book.)

Are you making bad decisions out of loneliness?

Nearly every unpartnered person gets lonely sometimes. If you long for more social interaction, you will do nearly anything to connect with other human beings. I think it's why so many people hang out in bars, Starbucks, or the library. (See "What's your 'need for affiliation'?" in the *Assessing Your Assets: Why You're A Great Catch* book) I didn't understand why anyone could get any work done in a coffee shop with the loud expresso machines and the constant bustle, but then I realized some people thrive on being near others, even if there's little interaction.

In dating, however, it can cause you to make some decisions that are not the best. While I encourage you to go to coffee with someone who sounds interesting but may not have a beguiling picture, if you're doing too many one-time-only coffee dates, you might be making your decision to meet out of loneliness, not out of interest.

Or worse, if you continue to see someone you know isn't a good match just because it's better than sitting at home, are you really doing either of you a service? If you are feigning romantic interest just to get out of the house, that is taking advantage of him.

If you tell him you aren't romantically interested, but would still like to hang out as friends and he agrees, that's fine. But if he harbors any hope for romance and you're clear you aren't into him that way, it's best to tell him. He may decide it is too difficult to be around you knowing his feelings are unrequited. Or he may decide to let those romantic feelings go and just be pals.

So instead of looking to dating to get your social needs met, try other outlets. Tag along with your pals as they do things they enjoy — exercise, classes, movies, theater. Even if you aren't as big a fan of the activity, you will get to hang out with them and have a new experience. Who knows, you might end up enjoying the new activity, and perhaps meet someone interesting in the process!

What's your definition of romance?

Often men say they are romantic in their online dating profiles. I've learned this means different things to different people. One may think that calling every day is romantic, while the other is expecting regular cards, letters, and candle-lit dinners.

It seems men and women often have different concepts of romance. This is so common, my friend Greg Godek has spawned an empire writing books on how to be romantic starting with *1001 Ways to Be Romantic*. I'm not sure how many men read these books, or if they are just purchased by their mates and left in obvious places where she hopes he'll read a few pages.

I've thought that any man truly interested in a woman he's met online would move to the head of the queue if he single red rosebrought just a single red rose to the first date. Corny? Perhaps. But I think men underestimate how such a gesture endears him to her. In fact, I think generally men underestimate how flowers of any kind melt most women's hearts. I've only received flowers from four men out of 91 — one bouquet on a first date, an arrangement on my 50th birthday, a single red rose on a first date, and a bouquet of tulips on a first date.

One evening while talking to a man I hadn't met yet although we've spent hours on the phone, I mentioned I hadn't had dinner. He said if he lived closer, he'd come fix me dinner or take me out. Later I thought it would be romantic if in that situation again, a guy called my local Chinese restaurant and had something delivered.

Or, again in a situation where we haven't met yet, but are getting close by phone, wouldn't it be heart-melting for him to send flowers? What would it cost — $25? — probably what he spent on lunch with pals. But the benefits would be many times greater than the cost.

As I discussed in "Instead of roses, he gives you ..lin-gerie," (in the *Real Deal or Faux Beau: Should You Keep Seeing Him?* book) some men think romance includes gifts and doing things for the woman he's wanting to woo. This can be great — if they are gifts the woman appreciates. And I think women also show affection by doing things she thinks her guy will like.

How do women show romance? I think women are more prone to light candles, draw bubble baths, send greeting cards and chill champagne glasses. Early in our courtship, I brought my ex flowers — something he said no other woman had ever done. After years of marriage, I put little love notes in his jacket and slacks' pockets when he was packing for a trip. He opened them throughout his boutonniere trip when he put his hand in a different outfit's pocket. When we were attending a formal affair, I always bought him a boutonnière, as I had within days of our meeting when we attended our first formal event together.

What do you do for your man that you think is romantic? What do you like to receive that you think is romantic?

A primer for how to become more romantic

In "What's your definition of romance?" (page 54) we talked about specific activities that most women consider romantic. I've been thinking more about what comprises romance. Then I got this question from a male Adventures in Delicious Dating After 40 reader:

> *I have some angst about Valentine's Day. It is a form of performance anxiety. I confess that I never prepare sufficiently, and it is always in the final hours that I find myself attempting to justify not having done anything creative or romantic. But at the last minute I am in the realization that something must be done. And so something is, but rarely is it a detailed and well-executed plan, more like heartfelt appreciation expressed with sincerity but insufficient investment to establish deep proof. And so there is anxiety about my performance. Will it pass cupid's muster?*
>
> *What is the practical way to become more romantic?*

What a great question!

Romance is all about showing your woman you've put some thought and effort into something you think would make her happy. So while your last-minute efforts show her you care, for the next event start thinking about it a month or so in advance. Put it on your calendar to just notice her and what she likes.

Take note if she says she likes a certain flower, smell, movie, food, book, color, etc. Or listen as she tells you about a friend's vacation or gift and says something like, "That sounds so wonderful."

Romance is about noticing

Romance is about noticing, then doing something to give her what you think she'd like. If she adores Italian food but a trip to Assisi isn't in the near future, how about giving her a big basket with favorite Italian food that you cook for her? Or a trip to a favorite, but not often frequented, Italian restaurant? It really doesn't have to be a big deal — the big deal is that you paid attention and made some true effort to please her.

He responded:

Yes, somehow I knew that more preparation would be the answer. In fact the prize usually goes to the one with the most preparation, especially when preparation is the primary evidence of consideration. I think many relationships wither because of one or the other being "inconsiderate." Just considering the other's wishes and pleasures is a great start toward mutual appreciation.

What do you think is the foundation of romance?

What dates are you inviting to influence you?

W ithin the first few weeks of the new year, I was contacted by five of the men I'd gone out with the last two years. I'd been thinking about how grateful I was that many good men had passed through my life as a result of dating. In fact, I told each of the five, "I'm grateful that we met and I have you now in my life," even though we are not romantic.

It reminded me of a saying a colleague often uses in his speeches. Professional speaker and author Charlie "Tremendous" Jones is known for quoting a speaker he heard 50 years ago who impacted his life. The speaker, whose name Charlie can't remember, said, "You are the same today that you will be five years from now except for two things — the people you meet and the books you read."

Let's take the first part, "the people you meet," and apply it to dating. Not all the potential suitors with whom you have coffee will have an influence on your life, but some can and will. Even if the encounter is not the best, you can learn from it. I know I approach relationships differently because of the men I've met through the dating adventure.

Secondly, he suggests we will be different because of the books we read. That quote was said before the Internet and many other media, so I'd say we can be impacted by the work of various authors, screen writers, playwrights, directors, etc. Maybe even bloggers. ☺

The key, I believe, is who are we inviting to influence us? If we have our dating filter set to allow interesting, thoughtful men through and weed out those who spell trouble, we will more likely allow in those who can help positively mold our thinking about relationships. If you read positive, abundance-focused writing, you're more likely to think more that way, thus attract more quality people and experiences into your life. If you only read about all men being players, cads, and losers, those are the ones you'll find asking you out.

Who are you inviting to influence you?

So who are you inviting to influence you? What books, blogs, sites, radio shows, TV shows, and movies are you allowing to shape your thinking and therefore your perspective on life and dating?

Being "in wonder" about your date's behavior

Have you ever wondered what a date was thinking when he said or did something not expected? I have. With various guys.

💜 My date said, "I hate to leave. I really wish I could stay with you longer." Then he sent a "Have a nice life" email a day later.

💜 He flirted with me online, wanting to take me to lunch, even knowing we had a friend in common and she would, no doubt, tell me he was married.

💜 We hadn't talked in months, yet he thought he could pick up where he'd left off with me.

💜 After sleeping over once, he said he'd like some drawer and closet space to leave a few things for next time.

💜 On a second encounter, I'd invited him over for coffee after a nearby evening meeting he attended. He brought his shaving kit, with the assumption he'd be staying over.

💜 After a nice coffee together one evening, my date didn't walk me to my car.

I've frequently heard myself ask, "What was he thinking?" when some behavior didn't match my expectation of normal. It's easy to get judgmental about behaviors that are different than you think are proper.

Relationship counselor Sonika Tinker taught me a different approach years ago. While I admit I don't engage in this inquiry 100%, I use it more than I used to.

The approach is to be "in wonder" about the behavior.

So instead of making him wrong for getting too chummy too fast, be curious. "I wonder what would make him think it was okay to put his hand on my knee within the first 10 minutes of our meeting?" When you engage in such questioning, you explore options, rather than making assumptions. Ideally, if you are close enough and can ask without sounding judgmental or irritated, get his take on the situation.

When my ex and I would engage in being "in wonder," we typically saw that our assumptions were wrong. When I thought he purposefully blew off my requests, the truth was he'd forget I'd asked if it wasn't written down. So instead of being affronted, I could help him manage his memory loss by making sure requests were

It doesn't prevent your exercising your "wonder" muscle

in writing. When he felt I was rude for interrupting him when telling me a story, by being in wonder he learned that I thought he was done sharing, so I jumped in. We worked on a signal to show he was done expressing a thought.

I know it can be hard to discuss things like this with a new guy. However, that doesn't prevent your exercising your "wonder" muscle. You can still be curious about any bothersome behavior and think of possible other interpretations, rather than a judgmental one.

So instead of thinking the guy who didn't want to leave was lying, by being in wonder I could see that another alternative was he felt that way in the moment, but then changed his mind upon a day's reflection.

See if you can think of some recent date's curious behavior and how you can be "in wonder" about it if you'd been judgmental.

When do you feel most vulnerable in dating?

Recently I've been feeling sort of vulnerable regarding the guy I've been seeing. He doesn't call every day and if more than a few days pass, I begin to feel he's gone "poof" like so many men before him. I could call him — and I have — but know that *He's Just Not That Into You* says if he doesn't call regularly, it can be a yellow flag.

It made me think of when many women feel vulnerable in dating.

♥ ***Immediately upon meeting a new guy*** — Most of us go through a little uncomfortableness immediately upon meeting a new guy as we want him to like us. We are told that men are visual, so if he doesn't like how we look, then the date can be awkward. In fact, it can be painful if the guy has few social skills and tells you quickly through his words or behavior that he's not attracted to you.

💜 ***After the first date when you want him to call*** — If you like him and want him to call, the next 24 hours can be excruciating until either he calls, you get distracted by other activities, or you give up on his calling. You can invest in a lot of emotion waiting for this call. Sometimes to head off agonizing you call him, although you know that is often not the best route. Even though some men like a woman making the next move, many see it as needy.

> *You can invest in a lot of emotion waiting for his call*

💜 ***Immediately after having sex for the first time*** — There's a physiological chemical release during sex and women often become more emotionally attached to their partner. If the guy understands this, it can lead to wonderful cuddling and conversation. However, if he doesn't, the woman can feel alone and abandoned.

💜 ***Within days of the first time having sex*** — For many, the first time is a sexual audition. If he says, "I'll call you" and he doesn't within the next 48 hours, she often feels she didn't pass and feels rejected.

💜 ***When you're not sure where you stand*** — You've been dating for a little while, yet there's been no sign that he thinks you two could be a steady relationship. He keeps calling you periodically to ask to get together, but you're not sure if it's out of loneliness or if he's into you. He continues to go online (you can see when he last logged on — today!), so you think he must not be completely satisfied with you.

Does this list match your experiences of vulnerable times? If not, what should I add? And when do you think men feel most vulnerable?

Beware the duplicity trap

Sometimes in dating (and in life) we choose not to reveal the whole truth. We don't lie, but we omit parts of the picture. The conundrum is whether telling the whole truth is best, including gnarly details we know will be disturbing to the other, or to reveal only what seems prudent.

I visited a dance club I'd heard about from a friend. He occasionally went there with a woman friend who he described having some very distinctive features.

Although my friend wasn't there, I spotted a woman who looked as he'd described his dancing buddy. I approached her and asked if she knew our mutual friend. Indeed she did. We chatted and she asked how he and I had met. I responded truthfully, "On Match.com." I went on to say that was several years ago and what a dear friend he has become, and we chatted about other things.

This morning I called and told my pal I'd met his

friend. He was surprised since she and I live an hour apart. I told him I had noticed her at the club and figured she might be the gal he'd told me about, so introduced myself. I also told him of her question to me and my response.

"Oh, crap!" (Actually, his response was more profane than that.) "She has no idea I've ever been on Match.com, nor that I was ever seeing other women."

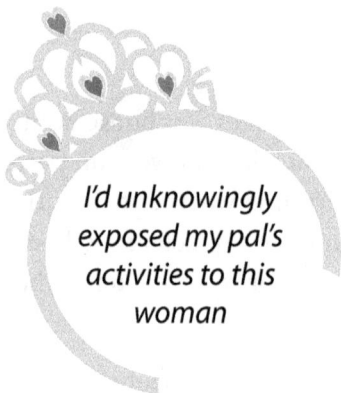

> *I'd unknowingly exposed my pal's activities to this woman*

My heart sank as I realized I'd unknowingly exposed my pal's activities to this woman, whom he'd always referred to as a friend, not someone he dated. He's a close confidant and I would never want to do anything that would cause him grief. Even though he was upset, he didn't blame me nor try to make me feel bad.

This event showed keenly how duplicity can bite you. He had his reasons for not telling her he was seeing others — just as I've had a "don't ask, don't tell" policy until a relationship heats up. However, although the unspoken code of online dating is "assume there are others," they did not meet online. So she'd have no reason to suspect there were other women. Did he have an obligation to tell her he was seeing others? Did she ever ask?

On the upside, my call alerted him so he could be thinking how he would discuss this with her, rather than being blindsided when they next spoke. On the downside, the cat is out of the bag, through not malice, just friendliness. I wouldn't have offered the Match.com info if she hadn't asked, and I responded truthfully, as I didn't see any need to lie since he described her as a friend.

When you multi-date without telling your dates that you are, you may be setting your own trap. Beware of your own wicked web you weave if you decide to be non-disclosing with someone you're seeing more than a few times. You never know who might unwittingly spring the trap.

Being in step with the dance of dating

A date and I met some gal pals and their hubbies at a zydeco dance club. If you're unfamiliar with this term, the music originated in southern Louisiana. Like most dances, there is a basic step, then embellishments as you get more comfortable.

None of us knew the steps so we arrived early for the lessons. Dancing alone to the calls of the instructor, the steps seemed easy — almost ridiculously so. We spent 30 minutes going over the basic steps and some easy variations.

But as soon as we coupled with a partner, things changed dramatically. Now we had to dance in union. And the transitions from one variation to another were particularly problematic for my date and me. It didn't make matters easier that he treated me as if I was inept, telling me, "In three steps we're going to change direction." I'm sure he thought he was being helpful. He was a newbie at this, too, so why was he acting as if I was unable to catch on? If he were just to lead properly, he wouldn't need to announce his intentions.

I was not having a good time. When the lessons were over, my date and I went to one of the tables ringing the room. We sat there for over an hour, without once dancing together again. The only dancing I did was with my gal pals who got tired of their men not wanting to dance either, so we group danced.

As I reflected on the evening and how I didn't take more control of having a good time, I thought of how dancing is like dating. (You knew I'd go there, didn't you?)

💚 ***Things are uncomplicated when you are alone.*** You don't have to worry about anyone else's rhythm, or which way they want to go. You don't have to give a second of concern over avoiding stepping on his toes, or zigging when he's zagging.

💚 ***It is much easier when you have an instructor.*** The caller made it so simple by telling us exactly which foot to put in front or back. Perhaps this is why we buy dating books and talk to our friends about what we should do — we like having guidance.

💚 ***Don't let someone else's attitude affect you.*** It is hard to have a good time if someone seems bent on being overly "helpful," which feels condescending. I could have — should have — ignored what I felt was patronizing, or told him he needn't talk to me that way.

💚 ***You create your own good time.*** Since my date seemed uninterested in dancing, I could have commandeered another willing gent. Men were continually walking around looking for partners. What prevented them from asking me was I wasn't dancing with anyone and was only seen next to my date. I could have easily asked one of them to dance, but I didn't. I stewed in my own juices instead of seeking a good time.

Cut your losses. I'd asked my date to dance several times, but he declined. After an hour of watching others dance, I suggested that we leave because he didn't seem to be enjoying himself, and I wasn't enjoying only watching others dance. He said, "We've only been here an hour and I didn't pay $26 (the entrance fee) for just an hour." I now realize I should have said I'd pay him back the $26 so we could leave and try to salvage some of the evening. Or I could have begun to ask others to dance. I did neither. I should have been more adamant about cutting the loss of the evening.

While dancing — and dating — can be a blast, it is so dependent on what you bring to the floor. If you are determined to have a good time, as my gal pals were, you can have one even if your partner isn't. Yes, it takes determination to have fun when you're with someone who doesn't seem to have the same goal. But it's not impossible if you are clear on enjoying yourself no matter what.

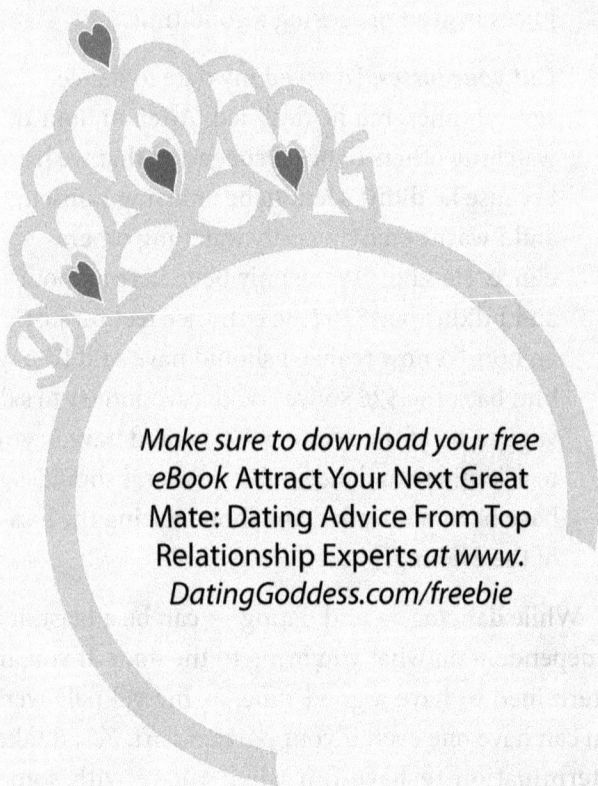

Make sure to download your free eBook Attract Your Next Great Mate: Dating Advice From Top Relationship Experts *at www. DatingGoddess.com/freebie*

Are you sending (or receiving) mixed messages?

Y ou know what mixed messages are, but you may not be aware you're sending them:

💜 You tell the guy you're dating you want to move slowly, yet you try to seduce him on the third date.

💜 You claim you like to cook, but when you invite him over for a DVD you always ask him to pick up takeout.

💜 You say you want a committed relationship and are only interested in dating him, but your on-line dating profile is still active.

💜 You tell him he's wonderful and are smitten by him, but you make no effort to introduce him to your friends.

You know how important words are. And you know how important actions are. But when words and actions don't match, we believe the actions. In college, studying non-verbal communication, we learned that good trial attorneys are trained to notice a witness' body language to discern if they were telling the truth or not.

So are you being congruent with your words and actions? Or is there a gap?

And what if he is sending mixed signals:

- He tells you how much he cares for you, but you hear from him only once a week. A lack of action (he doesn't call) is really an action (other things are taking his attention and priority).

- He says he really likes being with you, but he only asks you out once a week for midweek dates.

- He expresses how hot you are and how much he's attracted to you but he doesn't touch you nor try to kiss you, even after several dates.

Something is amiss.

If you become aware of your own inconsistencies between words and actions, sit down with a friend, counselor or note pad and ask yourself what's going on. Conflicting words and behaviors often exemplify conflicting attitudes.

- You think you should like him because all your friends say he's a nice guy. But you are always late to dates with him, even though you're punctual in all other areas of your life. Part of you doesn't really want to go out with him.

💗 You're saying what you think would make him happy or more attracted to you, but what you're saying isn't true. Knowing he has kids you say, "I love kids" even though you don't like being around them much.

💗 Part of you tells you that you should behave a certain way, or "women your age" should act a particular way. You are toned and fit, yet you wear matronly clothing and old-fashioned hair and make up because you don't want to appear too sexy.

And if it's he who's sending the clashing communications, gently point them out and ask him about it. He may get defensive or deny the incongruence. If he does, he's probably hiding something.

Are you date sated — or hungry?

Sate: satisfy (a desire or an appetite) to the full; supply (someone) with as much as or more of something than is desired or can be managed.

You know not to grocery shop when you are hungry as you'll be tempted to take home food that isn't really good for you.

The same is true in dating.

When you are "hungry" — lonely, bored, horny — you respond to or make contact with men who you normally wouldn't find appealing. You go on coffee dates with guys you know you don't have an ounce of interest in just for something to do. You may accept a second date invitation if he isn't odious. When you've had your dating "fill" you have to awkwardly disengage, declining additional dates, leaving the guy bewildered at what happened.

However, if you're seeing someone you like, even if it isn't serious, no one else looks appealing. If you receive regular emailed matches you automatically hit delete or give them a quick scan. No one entices you to respond or make contact. You are date sated.

You can also be disinterested in dating when you are satiated by other activities in life. If your appetite for affection, attention, and activities is quenched from other sources, you are not drawn to potential dates. You ignore winks, emails and maybe even phone calls. You have pushed yourself away from the dating table. You say, "Thank you, but I'm full."

Shortly after experiencing a difficult break up, I binged on my matches like a starving woman who hadn't had a morsel in months. I contacted men to whom I normally wouldn't have been drawn. I met them for coffee, and then had to send the "We're not a match" email afterwards. I was not being discerning — devouring everything that was put before me. And while I believe in experimenting, just like at a buffet, and at least "tasting" (meeting) men who are the least bit appealing, I guzzled coffee dates as if it were my last chance to meet anyone.

Notice how you feel about dating right now. Are you ravenous? Slightly hungry? Or satisfied? This will determine how you approach dating.

Be willing to retry activities you think you don't like

Part of the fun of dating is trying new things that your date suggests. If you have the attitude of "I don't like that" even though you haven't tried it for 10, 20, or 30 years, you'll kill the enthusiasm your date has for planning activities. And you'll deprive yourself of expanding your horizons.

Let's say your date suggests roller skating. The last time you roller skated was 20 years ago, and you remember your feet hurt and it was hard to stay upright.

But since then you've taken yoga and have better balance. You also have lost some weight and have stronger legs. But even if you've gained weight and have bad knees, why not experience it again and re-decide if you like it? You probably won't end up being a midlife roller derby star, but who knows if you might like it or not?

You're a different person now than you were 20 years ago.

You'll have fun in the exploration, especially if you explain to your date your reluctance and former opinion, but that you're willing to try it again. Get his agreement that you'll check in with each other after an hour and if your old decision still holds true and you're not having a good time, then he won't make you stay. Ask him to help you through your concerns and he'll probably be by your side helping you stand up — or get up when you fall. You'll learn a lot about him and how he approaches this activity knowing your unease. And I'm guessing there will be a lot of laughing, even if just for a short while until you determine if you like it or not.

> *You'll learn a lot about how he approaches this activity knowing your unease*

This retrying attitude extends beyond activities but can include food. Did you try sushi 20 years ago and didn't like it? But now you're ready to try some new things, or maybe you've expanded your palate into other international cuisines. So why not give it a try? I love trying new flavors with someone who's an expert. An Indian boyfriend asked my taste preferences, then ordered a scrumptious curry meal after I thought I didn't like Indian food.

Years ago, I decided I didn't like camping. I'm one of those gals who exemplifies the line, "Camping is staying in a hotel without room service." We'd camped on nearly all our childhood family vacations and while the scenery was breathtaking, it was cold, uncomfortable, and a chore. Although I love the outdoors and wanted to experience the back country, I knew I couldn't bear the weight of a full backpack. So I organized a llama back-country trip, where the llamas carried the gear. The llamareros (llama handlers) did much of the work, setting up our tents, blowing up air mattresses, cooking meals, rigging a solar shower and putting up a private privy. The scenery was unparalleled. I got to experience camping with a new perspective and am glad I did.

So the next time a date suggests something you haven't tried in a long time, tell him of your past experience but say you're willing to try it. Admit your concerns so he can help devise a way to mitigate them. And agree on an escape plan in case your previous decision is upheld.

Do your friends birddog for you?

By "birddog" I am not referring to Labrador Retrievers, English Pointers, or German Shorthaired Pointers. However, I am referring to their ability to find and point out what you are looking for.

The verb "birddog" is common in sales. When someone birddogs for you, s/he is providing you leads to prospects. When I was president of a sales association, we had "Birddog Breaks" at our meetings to share the kind of prospect we each were looking for, and other members would provide prospect contact info if they had it.

When your friends birddog for you, they are suggesting their single friends as possible romantic partners for you. They may do as little as providing a name, contact info, and a brief bio. Others may more actively birddog, playing a yenta role, inviting you both on an outing and talking you up to each other.

My point is, are you actively asking your friends to

birddog for you? Are you telling them you are dating and the type of guy you're looking for? Some people pooh-pooh the concept of friends setting you up for dates. But others know that the more people who are on the lookout for a great guy for you, the more likely you'll find them.

So share your quest with your pals and ask them to be on the lookout for you. Be specific with what you are looking for; otherwise, you'll be set up on blind dates with people they think are great but are in no way a good match for you. And always thank your friends for their efforts even if the date is a bust. Tell them what you liked about the guy and repeat what you're look-ing for so you can train your birddog to be an even better hunter.

Host a singles mingle

A pal is having a divorce party soon when his paperwork is final. His divorce was amicable, so he would be celebrating his new-found singledom. I suggested it might be fun to turn it into a singles mingle event.

He: "That would be boring, as I'd have a house full of guys."

DG: "You don't know any single women?"

He: "Not many. I've been married for a while!"

DG: "Tell your friends to bring single women."

He: "Like they know any. That's why we hang out together! None of them can get dates!"

DG: "I heard an idea where your ticket into the party is to bring a single person of the opposite sex who you think is great, but isn't a match for you." (I heard about this idea a long time ago, but then it was featured in a "Sex and the City" episode.)

He: "So you bring someone you dated but it didn't work out?"

DG: "It could be someone you dated, or it could just

be a friend you think is terrific, but not for you."

He: "Does it need to be someone interested in dating?"

DG: "Well, that's the purpose. I wouldn't bring a guy I knew wasn't interested in dating."

He: "Could they bring folks who can't get a date?"

DG: "You want to have a house full of terrific people, not those with low social skills."

He: "But could I also invite my coupled friends? They're my friends, too and I want to be able to invite them to the party."

DG: "Sure. You could have a way of signifying who was available and who wasn't. Maybe a red dot on their shirt for "taken" and a green one for "available.""

He: "Well, this is sounding more interesting with the prospect of some interesting, hot women to balance my buds."

DG: "Maybe you'll invite me!"

Have you been to a party like this? If so, how did it work?

Are you out of his league — or he yours?

"I'm out of your league" sounds so snooty, snotty, and superior. You're looking down your nose at the other, saying he isn't good enough for you.

A potential suitor once emailed me, "You're so far out of my league that I wouldn't be allowed in the stadium where your league plays. I can only play in the fantasy league for your league. I can't even park in your league's parking lot." Clearly, thinking someone is out of your league is not starting from a position of strength.

By proclaiming someone is not in your league, are you cutting out some great guys? Absolutely. Might some of them be a good fit for you? Perhaps. We hear about these kind of mismatched relationships all the time.

What are we really saying with "out of your league"? That you don't match on some significant level. It could be a marked difference in socio-economic or education backgrounds, or intelligence. Often this refers to big differences in physical attractiveness. A Ph.D. professor may not be a match with a fast-food worker. Or a country-club type won't be good long-term with a laborer. Of course, there are always exceptions.

I've dated men with different economic or educational levels from mine. While I may have enjoyed the guy's company, as we got to know each other, the discrepancies emerged. His vocabulary, pronunciation, or even table manners showed our different backgrounds, expectations and standards. While I try to embrace men from different walks of life, if there are too many things that have a wide gap, it can be a strain. And perhaps some men went "poof" because they felt I wasn't in their league.

> *Perhaps some men went "poof" because they felt I wasn't in their league*

What to do if you find yourself with someone who is in a different league? As long as you are playing the same game (wanting romance), and have the same team goal (enjoying being with each other), who cares if he's National League and you're American League? If you want to find a way to play together, you will. And if you find that one of you is major league and the other on a farm team, one of you will strike out.

Do you give your date grace?

I mean grace in this sense: mercy, clemency, lenience, pardon, consideration, kindness, compassion, forgiveness, courteous goodwill.

At the beginning of any relationship, there are ups and downs. In "What's your date's score on the Delight/Disappointment Scale?" (in the *Real Deal or Faux Beau: Should You Keep Seeing Him?* book) I discuss how you want to notice when your date delights and disappoints you. The point is not to jettison him the first time he disappoints, but to notice it and give him some grace. We all have off days. However, if your disappointments far outweigh the delight, ponder moving on.

I've been surprised when I've heard women's stories of dumping a guy they've been seeing after the first miscommunication. I can understand if he's lied or cheated. Those are zero-tolerance situations. But women have cut the cord on a guy the first time he is late, without giving him a chance to explain. That is cold. If it is a recurring pattern, then yes, something must be said and modified — either his lateness or her expectation of the time he'll appear.

I tend to give any man I'm dating a lot of grace. Sometimes perhaps too much. I tend to forgive hiccups that I know other women would bail for. I work to live by that maxim about treating others as I would like to be treated. But there is a limit to my tolerance. If a man violates my trust a second time, he's gone. Sometimes he's gone the first time, depending on how egregious the violation.

Luckily, I've only had a few arguments with men I've dated. In each instance, if he is angry at me it feels like he hasn't given me any grace. From his comments, he allows me no slack to be human, nor any consideration that my motivation is different than his negative interpretation. No grace.

Can a relationship blossom without grace? I don't think so. Humans make mistakes. We say insensitive things, have trouble hiding our less-than-positive feelings, choose the wrong words, and take things personally. If your budding relationship is grace deficient, it will wither and die soon.

Can a relationship blossom without grace?

The place to start is with your own grace be-

havior. Don't expect it from him until you practice it yourself. If you need some reminders on how to do this, see "Turn your liabilities into assets" (in the *Assessing Your Assets: Why You're A Great Catch* book; apply the concept to his behaviors that drive you batty), "Ignore dating rule #1 at your peril," (in the *Date or Wait: Are You Ready for Mr. Great?* book) and "Being 'in wonder' about your date's behavior," (page 65).

In fact, you can begin to strengthen your grace muscle on strangers, family members and coworkers. Next time someone cuts you off in traffic, instead of honking, try taking a deep breath and saying grace. But instead of saying grace as you would at the start of a meal, try thinking "I give you grace" to that person who is obviously not fully present to how his/her behaviors affect others. Besides, honking won't change their behavior (see Ignore dating rule #1 at your peril).

The worst two words in dating

Here are a few examples of two-word phrases you don't really want to hear while dating:

Comb over

Hair plugs

Spousal reconciliation

I'm married

It's over.

None of these would be music to your ears. Some of these are worse than the phrase I want to focus on:

"I've decided…"

These two words are rarely followed by something positive, although conceivably they could be coupled with "…you're the one for me" or "…I'm in love with you" or "…I can't live without you."

More often, though, they are followed with "…this

isn't working," "…I don't think we should see each other any more," "…we'd be better as just friends," or "…I can't continue seeing you anymore."

The reason these words are so upsetting is that you haven't been given the respect of being included in a discussion leading up to "I've decided." This is understandable if you've only been seeing the other a short time.

However, I've heard these words most often when I've been seeing the person a month, two or more. "I've decided" did not follow a spat or difficult time, so it seemed to come out of thin air. There was no heart-to-heart discussion about the other being unhappy, or what he wanted that I wasn't providing. He made a decision and I was out on my ear, period.

Of course, two adults have the freedom to change their minds about a relationship at any time. But it seems that the longer you've been seeing someone (or been married to them!), you should at least be privy to a conversation about what isn't working or what the other wants before the "I've decided" pronouncement. Not that his mind would be changed, but it seems more respectful to be engaged in the process. Perhaps the decision was based on a misinterpretation of a comment, and it would give you an opportunity to clear it up. But once "I've decided" has been uttered, it is virtually impossible for him to reconsider.

What do you think about "I've decided"? And what other two words can you think of that are difficult to hear when dating?

If you're in the public eye, be careful how you behave in dating

Sometimes I get flummoxed by how people behave. I wonder, "What would motivate someone to…" or "How could they possibly think that this behavior is acceptable…" or "Doesn't she have a clue how this would affect her reputation?"

I'm even more flummoxed with people's — okay, men's — behavior in dating. I'm sure women do bizarre things, but I'm not as privy to those.

For example, two years ago a nice-looking man kept coming up at the top of my matches on Match. com. After a month, I emailed him a note, mentioning the things we had in common. Nothing. A few months later he comes up as the #1 match on Yahoo! Personals. I again launched a salvo, different than the first. Over the next year, I sent two or three emails just to see if he'd respond. Nothing.

Eight months ago, I saw his picture — the same one he used in his online profile — in a Realtor's ad. He worked 3 blocks from me! Soon after that I was at a friend's business club. Everyone introduced themselves to the group of 150. I heard his name and thought, "I must introduce myself to him by my online handle and see if he has any memory of my emails." By the time the introductions were over, he'd left.

Your actions have repercussions beyond the dating world

I emailed him a short note, "Sorry we didn't get to meet at the club" to his office address. I shared nonjudgmentally that I'd emailed him from the dating sites, but hadn't heard back, and that he worked in my neighborhood. He responded perfunctorily.

Was I being a stalker? Not really. The emails were short and infrequent. It was clear he had no interest in me, but it became a game to see if he would respond. However, the last email told all. It's easy to ignore someone when you don't run in the same circles. But I could have easily become a business asset to him if he'd had a more pleasant response to my email — even a polite "Thanks but we're not a match." I regularly hear of people wanting to move out of or into my neighborhood. Might he have benefited from another person sending him leads?

Now whenever I see his ad or sign in a yard, I think, "I'd never refer that guy any business. He doesn't know the basics about how to treat people." After all, how hard would it have been for him to respond to any of my dating site emails? Not hard at all. But then when he found out I was at his club and in his area, he could have said something like, "I'm seeing someone right now, so am out of the dating market. But if you're interested, I'd love to have coffee just to get to know you and see how we might help each other's businesses." Networking 101.

So if your profession puts you in front of the public, know that your actions have repercussions beyond the dating world.

Why listening is so seductive

A guy pal told me about a woman in a weekly group activity he attends who has become enamored with him and it makes him uncomfortable. When I asked what makes it uncomfortable he said, "I'm not at all attracted to her. She's too effusive. She is always telling the others how I'm the first man in her life who has really listened to her."

This skill is somewhat rare. People — even good friends — can go through the motions of listening. They do the right things: eye contact, head nodding, saying "uh huh," "I see," "yes." But this phrase describes them best: "The porch light is on, but nobody's home."

They aren't truly listening. How do you know? Because they ask you something a few minutes later that you've already stated. They were going through the motions to appear the attentive listener. But they weren't really present. Perhaps they were thinking of a good story to tell you about what you just said, or a question to ask you, or heaven forbid, what they want for dinner.

But this guy is a good listener. He shows he's listening. He makes relevant comments or asks related questions. He may throw in his own stories, but it's a give and take. I never feel he's hogging the conversation or ignoring me.

And he remembers — for the next day, several days or even over a week. This is an anomaly in my experience. My ex could barely remember what I said once I was finished, and rarely the next day. And I'm not one of those nonstop talkers who prattle on. I'm very conscious of only sharing what I think would be of interest to the other, and then as truncated as I can be without the details unless he probes.

Listening well can be alluring. But how you listen says a lot about you and the importance you place on the speaker. I can be a lousy listener if I don't respect the speaker. Tom Peters said, "The highest compliment you can pay a customer is to listen." This applies to someone you're dating as well.

In my communication workshops I say, "If you change your listening, you change your relationships." If you start listening to someone who you've previously half listened to, it will shift how they experience you. I can nearly guarantee it will be for the better.

So are you a good listener to your dates? How do you make sure you listen well, even with the distractions of loud restaurants or bars or even Starbucks blending beverages?

Avoid frivolous talk on a date

Frivolous: unworthy of serious attention; trivial; of little value.

One of the consistent complaints men make about women is their incessant talking. And it's just not that there is no silence. But women more than men talk and talk and talk about things of no consequence to the men. In fact, she will go into great detail about people he doesn't know and will never meet. And the stories have no point that is relevant to him or her.

Women bond through talking. A woman talks to share part of her life with her man, which is why so much discussion is about people in her life — or even people she's never met but are in her friends' lives! Women also talk to sort out their opinions and feelings. "Talking it out" is a common habit

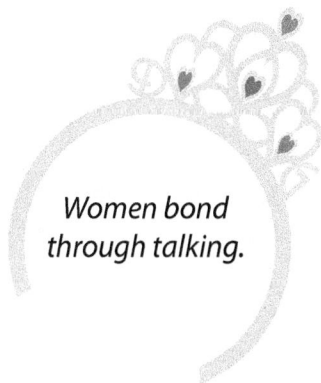

Women bond through talking.

109

among many women, and can provide release of tension.

The problem is women don't know with whom this is acceptable behavior and with whom it is an irritant. On a date — especially on early dates with a guy — it can be deadly. He wants to listen to you (if he's at all conscious), but if you babble on and on, he'll turn off quicker than a triggered safety valve. And if they end up in a relationship, she'll complain that he doesn't listen. Could it be that she rarely says anything relevant to him? Or things important to her are hidden beneath so much noise he doesn't know to listen up?

"And then he said…then she said…and then…and then…" and on and on. The man is thinking, "Get to the point!" Or she says, "Gina's boyfriend's cousin was so upset because…." He doesn't know Gina, her boyfriend or his cousin, so couldn't care less. Or she keeps talking and talking, saying little of consequence, perhaps even repeating herself.

I've noticed this in a lot of women and fight hard to not fall into this behavior, although I'm sure I do sometimes. But a decade ago I had an experience that made me realize how much frivolous talk I contributed. It cured me of much of it.

I attended a nine-day residential personal growth workshop. We'd been told that this workshop could be life-changing if we followed the guidance of our facilitators while we were there. I decided to participate full out — no holding back or deciding which processes I'd participate in and which ones I wouldn't. I trusted these leaders so I did the exercises fully.

The first day we were told there was to be no frivolous talk for the next three days. In fact, there was to be no talk at all outside of our workshop room, other than to discuss logistics (e.g., carpooling). We were to be silent.

I was struck by how many times I'd think of chatting with my classmates about unimportant things — the weather, her pretty jacket, could he pass the salt. I saw how much "noise" I contributed. These things weren't really important, or I didn't need to speak to communicate them.

By forcing us into silence, we saw how little of our usual babble really needed to be said. When the silence was lifted, we were much quieter than we'd been before. When we did speak, it was to ask a deeper question, or to share a meaningful insight.

We saw how little of our usual babble really needed to be said.

Although I've drifted back into some chatter, I talk less now than before. If someone asks me to repeat something that I then realize was unimportant, I say, "I'm just talking here — not saying anything."

Why don't you try observing and curbing your frivolous talk? You don't have to be silent, but think about what you say before you say it. Ask yourself, "Does this really need to be said? Will it make a difference to my listener?" If not, then button it up!

Men appreciate silence — especially if he's driving in heavy traffic or bad weather, or when first sitting down at a restaurant. Your smile will tell him you aren't giving him the "silent treatment," but just enjoying his company.

Cruising at festivals

O ur neighborhood is hosting a city-wide Italian festival today, so I decided to use it as an opportunity to cruise for men. After all, I'd heard how hanging out where people you are likely to like in the "real" world (vs. Internet) is a better option. So I wanted to experiment to see if this might work.

I like Italian men (and Greek, French, American, African, Brazilian, English, Spanish, German and ... men — do you see a pattern?). So where best to meet them outside of Italy? An Italian festival. Granted, most of them are not directly from Italy, but of Italian lineage. No matter — although I do love accents. I still like the general look of Italian guys. So where best to hunt them than in a gathering place for them? And not just an Italian bar or bocce ball court — but a much larger gathering. Kind of like fishing in a stocked lake versus a stream.

So I set out, balancing trying to look cute with comfortable shoes and clothes. Not the best bait, but it was what would work for an afternoon of walking in the sun. I just didn't see clomping on asphalt in heels and a skirt as the best choice.

I strutted (can you strut in sneakers?) down the street, taking in not only the crafts booths and cannoli vendors, but eyeing those partaking in the exhibits. There were men (and women) of all ages, body types and ethnicities, predominantly of Mediterranean extraction, as we would guess. I paused to people-watch while enjoying my Italian sandwich, listening to the accordion player on one side and the opera singers on the other. But no cute middle-aged prospects appeared. Not even any cute younger or older ones!

At the Vespa dealer display, I noticed a midlife, dark-haired, olive-skinned cutie. I immediately fantasized us riding off together, me perched on the back, like in an old movie. As he started his demo for a few onlookers, I moseyed over to see if I could flirt. Drat! A wedding ring.

On to the bocce ball court. If I took a lesson, maybe I'd attract a prospect. But the current pre-pubescent-boy players were starting a series so it looked like it would be a while before I'd get a turn. I passed.

The good news: I enjoyed a beautiful autumn day outside with entertainment, crafts/art to enjoy, and yummy Italian food, all within a few blocks of my house, and for less than $10 (for lunch). The bad news: No prospects. But hey, you can't always hit a bulls eye the first time out!

Will I try again at another festival? Yes. In fact, there's a Greek festival coming up. I love Greek dancing, Greek food, and of course, Greek men.

Mistaking nice for interest

 One of the hardest things in dating is when one of you misinterprets the other's niceness or politeness for interest. I've been on both sides — the misinterpreter and the misinterpreted. Last night I was on the latter side. Neither feels good.

I'd made an exception to my "coffee-only" first date rule and agreed to meet for dinner. He was sweet and a gentleman during the several get-to-know-you phone calls and we were both traveling an hour to meet. So insisting on just coffee seemed harsh.

From the calls I knew that for all his sweet disposition and growing fondness of me, I doubted we were a match. Yet, having experienced seeming pre-date mismatches turn into beaus, I thought "what the heck" and accepted his dinner invitation.

When I approached our meeting spot I could see that his profile pictures were about 10 years younger than the balding, slightly stooped 49-year-old man before me. Okay. People often look different than even recent pictures portray.

He was sweet and considerate as we walked the downtown district looking for an enticing restaurant. We decided on an unusual ethic cuisine. We enjoyed the stellar food and service as we chatted about life. He was an acceptable conversationalist, periodically asking about my interests or life, and only interrupting occasionally. I asked about him and offered my stories and information that pertained.

Throughout dinner, he peppered his comments with "I'd love to take you to…" or "We could go to…." It was clear he was hungry for a life companion and he hoped that would be me. Since I didn't share his perspective, I did not encourage him when he let those comments drop.

After dinner, he suggested we stroll and explore the shops and galleries. He stumbled to help me with my coat; clearly this was not something he had done a lot. He grabbed my hand telling me how much he'd looked forward to this night. Feeling uncomfortable holding hands with a man I knew didn't interest me, I gently dropped hands to button my coat. He put his arm around my shoulders. I switched my purse to the inside hand so it would not be easy to grab again, and lengthened the distance between us so it would not be easy to put his arm around me.

How does one gracefully dissuade a man from making advances? Aside from overtly saying something, which seemed hurtful and ungrateful after his treating for a splendid dinner, I did what I thought were enough signals for him to get the message. He didn't. In retrospect, I suppose I could have said, "I'm uncomfortable with PDAs on a first date," although if I'm into a guy that's not true.

He asked, "So do you see yourself dating a man from (his city)?" I know this was a perfect opening for me to say, "no," but that just felt mean. So I stammered something about being geographically undesirable. Ugh! For someone who usually considers herself to be forthright and articulate, I was coming up with nothing!

At my car we started to hug goodbye but he kissed me. I quickly broke it off and just hugged him. He held me longer than I'd have preferred and then kissed me again. I broke it off. He said, "Would you like to do this again?" I felt his loneliness, his pent-up craving to have someone in his life, but I could not agree to it. As nicely as I could, I uttered a noncommittal, "We can discuss it on the phone." and got in my car.

I wondered if I should have been blunt with him since he was not catching my distancing clues. It just seemed cruel to do so. However, I know it is also cruel to let someone have false expectations. I will tell as gently and compassionately as I can on the phone that we are not a match.

Nice guys don't have to finish last

I have an inkling into why the cliché "nice guys finish last" has become an axiom. Nice is not enough for many women to find a midlife man appealing.

I'm not suggesting that rude, obnoxious jerks are to be tolerated. But a man who's nice — and only nice — is not enough. At least not for me.

Despite the myth that nice guys are hard to find, in my dating adventure I've met lots of nice men. They are affable, pleasant, agreeable, kind, even generous and thoughtful. But these traits are just the starting point for me to be interested in a guy. If a man lacks these qualities, he's not for me. I need "nice plus."

What does it take for a man to go beyond nice? Some combination of confidence, humor, personality, passion (for something in addition to sex), intelligence, integrity, introspection, curiosity, thought-provoking conversation. He needs to be "up to something" in the world, whether making a difference in his neighborhood, with his work, or through a charity to which he contributes time in addition to money. He puts effort towards more than his own workouts and watching his favorite sports teams.

In my dating experience I've encountered lots of nice men. However, during our conversation, if nothing was divulged that made me interested in getting to know them more, we do not move forward. Perhaps I haven't asked the right questions; perhaps they were too modest to share how they single-handedly built 20 houses for homeless families or volunteered every Saturday to mentor troubled youth. Yet for the men who've intrigued me, they let slip that they are active in pursuits that contribute to others beyond their families. They are confident yet humble. They are proud of their accomplishments but not braggadocious.

How do you uncover if a man is more than just nice? Ask him questions about what he's committed to, excited about, or passionate for. Probe what makes him jump out of bed in the morning. Uncover what makes him most happy. (His answers need to be more than "You," although some smooth-talkers may try to sidetrack the questioning with that answer.) And you need to be prepared with your answers should he ask you the same.

Sometimes we are seduced by nice if we haven't had a man be kind or considerate to us in a while, and especially if our last man didn't treat us with much regard. Only you can decide if nice is enough for you.

Men's fear: she's a poser

Talking about dating with a midlife single friend he asked, "Do you know men's biggest dating fear?"

"Dating a psycho?"

"No."

"Getting an STD?"

"No."

"She gets pregnant?"

"Those are all high on the list, but it's not what I'm thinking of."

"Well, many women's fear is abandonment, but I doubt that's men's fear."

"It's not."

"What then?"

"That the woman he's falling for is a poser."

"You mean that she pretends to be someone she's not?"

"Sort of. When you're dating, a woman says she loves to watch sports. So you snuggle up together to watch football, basketball, whatever. She's right next to her man while reviewing the ESPN highlights. You take her to live games. Or she says she loves your favorite kind of food, your friends, your mother. But then, when you're thinking 'This has to be the most amazing woman on the planet,' and you fall head over heels for her, things start to change."

"Like what?"

"You discover she's just been pretending. She's really not into sports, your friends, family or food. She's just been going along with you thinking it will make you like her more. By the time you discover it, you've moved in together and now extricating yourself is very difficult."

"And you feel duped."

"Exactly. So now I know to hang out longer before making the plunge. See how she is over time, after the trying-to-impress-you phase lapses."

While this man felt that this behavior was prevalent in women, I can see it happens in both genders. I've had men suggest movies that later I learned they loathed, but they knew I wanted to see. I think it's our wanting to make a positive impression so we're flexible and amenable to doing what they want. The challenge is when that impression is seared into their thinking that's how you always are or what you like.

For example, I rarely drink. I may have one drink a month, and then only socially, often on a date. I'm not a teetotaler; I just know I have low tolerance so I don't regularly imbibe.

A man I dated for months brought me a gift of a bottle of port. Knowing he liked to have a glass in the evening, I'd bring it out when he was over and join him. After a few months of this behavior, he sat me down and said, "I'm concerned that you always seem to need a drink when I'm around. I'm hoping you can enjoy my company without needing alcohol to loosen up."

I was shocked. I was only having a glass to join him. I didn't "need" alcohol to be comfortable. He'd formed an opinion on why I did something based on only his limited observation — which is what nearly all of us do. I was grateful he brought it up so I could share my perspective.

Was I being a poser? In a way, yes. Since I rarely drink, I was "posing" as someone who drank regularly because I had a glass of port when he was around. Did I do it to make him like me more? Perhaps. I did it to share an activity I knew he liked, just like I agreed to accompany him to exotic restaurants, even though they wouldn't have been my choice. And he went to foreign films because he knew I enjoyed them, even though he wouldn't have chosen them on his own.

So where's the line between pretending to like something and agreeing to participate in something you know the other likes? I think you need to verbalize what's going on: "I wouldn't normally choose an Ethiopian restaurant, but I know you love the cuisine so I'd like to try it with you." "Spending Sunday watching football is not how I typically spend the day, but I want to be with you so will watch it with you today."

I think you have to strike a balance between only doing what you want and a willingness to try what your honey likes. If it is odious to you, share that you know he likes it, but you'd rather find things that you both enjoy. Or compromise like snuggling on the couch during the game, but you read with earphones playing music you like.

Where do you think is the line between pretending to like something you don't really, therefore being a poser, and wanting do be agreeable about joining your sweetie in activities you know he likes and you only tolerate?

Biggest surprise with midlife dating

I'm often asked, "What's the biggest negative surprise you've had with dating midlife men?"

Myanswer? Lack of conscientiousness.

This takes in several behaviors, all, coincidentally, starting with "c"!

💜 Lack of consideration.

I was emailed today, on the day of a dinner date, by a man canceling telling me he'd decided to be exclusive with another woman. It wasn't his exclusivity that bothered me, but that he didn't have the consideration to communicate the cancellation via a mode that guaranteed I'd get it. What if I was in appointments all day and didn't get the email? Calling would have been the preferred method, but I imagine he envisioned a difficult conversation, so took the easiest way out for him. The coward's way out.

Perhaps since he hasn't met me, he didn't feel he needed to treat me with much regard. However, if a man is interested enough in a woman to invite her to a nice dinner, wouldn't he have enough respect for her to treat her considerately, even if to cancel? My guess is that this is how he treats others, even though he has a senior-level position with a high-ranking politician. So he must know how to earn someone's respect. But perhaps he's so talented others overlook his lack of personal consideration. I'll never know.

Lack of consideration plays out over and over. Are midlife men really so self-absorbed that they have no clue how their lateness, last-minute cancellations, and texting difficult conversations, affect the other person? How disrespectful it feels? Are they missing the thoughtfulness gene? Or were they never taught (or have forgotten) manners? (To be fair, I'd guess there are many midlife women who behave similarly.) Shouldn't we be able to act like mature adults at this point?

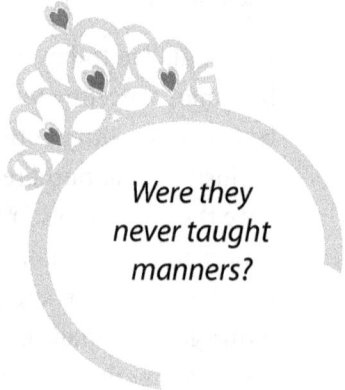

Were they never taught manners?

💜 Lack of consciousness of how to make a good impression.

Men show up for first dates late without calling, or in wrinkled garb, or take phone calls. Their online profiles are rife with sun glasses- and baseball hat-wearing pictures, often taken from many yards away. How can they possibly think this is appealing and representing them in the best possible way?

Do men really think that on a phone call or coffee date spending 90% of the time talking about themselves is attractive? I understand that they are in "impress her" mode, but are they so clueless that they don't understand that she'll be way more impressed if he seems to be interested in her life?

💜 Lack of courage (see #1).

This can be as simple as picking up the phone after a few dates and telling you that you're not a good fit for each other. Or telling you he's found someone he thinks is a better match. Or he's decided to go back to his wife/gf. Whatever the news, have the courage to confront it head on, not hiding behind an IM, text or email. In person is best, but even a phone call is better than electronic communication. I believe men convince themselves it will sting less to receive the missive via text, etc., but it's really because they don't want to have to face the perceived difficult conversation. We are adults. We have to have difficult conversations. It's called "maturity."

So maybe my real answer is, I'm surprised at some chronologically mature men's lack of maturity!

I did not intend this to come across as man bashing, as I'm sure we could change the pronoun in every sentence and men would agree that they've experienced some midlife women behaving the same way.

So the question to you is, what has negatively surprised you about dating midlife? I don't want to encourage a rant-fest, but more of a "this surprised me" dialog.

Why the "Golden Rule" melts down in dating

P eople often say they treat others as they want to be treated. But in dating (and in life) that frequently results in disappointment, hurt and anger.

Let's examine some common scenarios:

You write an email to a man whose online profile is appealing. He writes back, "Thanks, but we aren't a match." You're irritated thinking he is an insensitive jerk as you'd have preferred no response than a negative one. He acted how he'd like to be treated — telling you directly.

After a couple of dates with a guy, you decide you're really not interested him. You figure it is kinder just not to return his calls and he'll get the message, just as you prefer when a man loses interest he just stops making contact. He thinks you're incredibly rude to not communicate directly as he does when he's not interested in continuing with a woman.

A man you've been dating for a few months likes to text you, even long conversations. He even texts you concerns he has about the relationship. You think it is unbelievably immature to not pick up the phone to discuss these things, or better yet to tell you in person.

These examples are all of someone acting how they would want to be treated and the receiver thinks it's totally inappropriate. So what can you do?

My friend Tony Alessandra, Ph.D. is the author of *The Platinum Rule: Discover the Four Basic Business Personalities and How They Can Lead You to Success.*. In it Tony explains that the Platinum Rule is when you treat others how they want to be treated, not

> *How we want to be treated is not necessarily how others want to be treated.*

how you want to be treated. Because how we want to be treated is not necessarily how others want to be treated. He's right.

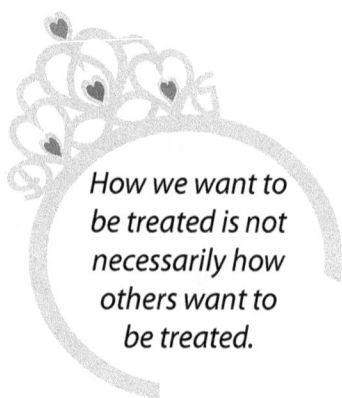

In dating it's hard to know how the other person wants to be treated until you get to know him some. And then even when you do know, where's the balance between always being conscious of the other's preferences and trying to honor them versus just being yourself? Constant vigilance gets wearisome.

The keys are 1) communication and 2) compromise. You can't always treat someone exactly how they want to be treated, nor should any of us expect that. But when something is unacceptable to you, see if you can tell him without seething, trying to understand his perspective. Tell him how it feels to you and see if you can come up with a mutually acceptable compromise. And allow him to not remember this bargain 100% of the time. But as long as he seems to be making a concerted effort, give him some grace.

A sensitive stomach can help you date better

I have a "sensitive" stomach. It helps me date better.

Why?

It's probably not what you think. It has more to do with men and less to do with food.

Having a delicate digestion makes me think through what I eat before I eat it. While I love the taste of fried foods, sausage and spicy dishes, I don't love how they make me feel afterward. Within minutes of eating this flavorful fare, my stomach is uncomfortable, sometimes to the point of queasiness, nausea — or worse.

I've learned not to eat foods that are tasty but come back to haunt me.

I bet you're ahead of me on how this makes me date better.

When I've encountered an initially delicious guy

— good looking, interesting conversation, sexy — I've been seduced into partaking in his temptations too soon. This may mean kissing earlier than usual, falling under his spell and getting attached too early, or doing things that feel good in the moment. But nearly always there is a price to pay — often pretty quickly.

His lip-smacking scrumptiousness comes back on me and makes me feel bad. I've indulged in something that felt good in the moment but quickly turned to an unhealthy aftermath — usually emotional, but sometimes coupled with physical maladies (upset stomach, crying, tight muscles from stress over him).

Now I've learned to put the brakes on and ask myself, "How will I feel about myself afterward? Will I feel better or worse?" More often than not, this allows me the distance to admit, "worse" and hold off on what I think will be so luscious now. There may be great evidence that it will be delectable. But if I wait until I'm more certain that all the ingredients are there to make it exquisite, I will have fewer experiences of heart burn and heartache.

You may say, "We aren't getting any younger. These mouthwatering opportunities are few and far between. Go for it! Seize the day!" Yes, there is that attitude. But my experience is there's always another opportunity to have something succulent that doesn't end up leaving your stomach and heart in a knot. Being willing to check on what your body and heart want is a step toward getting it long term and rejecting quick hedonistic urges that leave you feeling lousy afterwards.

Getting your cute on

The other day, while preparing for a second date (dinner at a nice restaurant) with a special guy, it occurred to me how much date prep differs significantly between genders. No big revelation here. But the "ah ha" was how little I think one appreciates what the other does.

OK, really, I was thinking how little men understand and appreciate what a women does to prepare for a nice date with a guy she likes.

When a man recently emailed me on the date day to cancel, I thought about how most men don't have a good picture of what many women do to prep for a date. I'd gone out of my way to do things I'd do at some point, but had some urgency because of the upcoming date with someone I felt was special (e.g., manicure, pedicure, curl hair, ensure outfit was clean and in good repair). So I spent extra time and money in prep for the date. I felt irritated that he didn't bother to communicate to me more in advance since he knew days before that he was going to be out of town on our date day. I would have postponed some of my activities.

A man's prep seems to include the following, starting with the basics and escalating the more he wants to impress her:

Show up within 15 minutes of the agreed upon time

Spray breath freshener/eat mint/brush teeth

Don a clean shirt

Comb hair

Refresh cologne/after shave

Shave again (assuming a late-in-the-day date and a heavy growth)

Change clothes entirely

Shower again

Ensure condoms are in wallet

Buy something to bring her (e.g., flowers, card, CD)

Call or text her the day before to confirm plans

Make reservation at restaurant

A woman's prep includes the following, starting with the basics and escalating the more she likes him:

Show up within 15 minutes of the agreed upon time

Spray breath freshener/eat mint/brush teeth

Don a clean top

Apply or refresh makeup and perfume

Do hair (self or by a stylist), including washing, dying, and/or curling/straightening

Change clothes entirely, including changing into sexy lingerie

Shower again

Depilate (self or by a esthetician) various body parts

Get manicure (self or by a manicurist)

Get pedicure (self or by a manicurist) if toes show in shoes

Get outfit dry cleaned or shop for new outfit/purse/shoes

Obsess about what to wear that is flattering and is sexy enough without looking like a slut

Call girlfriends and tell them about upcoming date, where he's taking you, his history, your feelings about him and get advice on what to wear.

> *A woman can take from an hour to a week to prepare for a date.*

A woman can take from an hour to a week to prepare for a date, depending on how much she likes the guy, wants to make a good impression, and where they are going. If it's a fancy event, it's like she's going to be on the red carpet. She wants to look and feel picture perfect. Even for a lunch or dinner date, she'll go though a number of the items outlined above. Rare is a woman wanting to make a good impression who doesn't spend at least some time renewing her make up, fussing with her hair, and thinking about her attire.

Unless you're one of those rare women who looks stunning with no makeup and can show up in rags and still make heads turn, what else do you do to prep for a date with a special guy? And guys, what did I forget from your list?

Musician hits sour

note

We'd intermittently flirted by email and phone for almost a year. We lived thousands of miles from each other so promised we'd let the other know when we'd be nearby. He toured in a popular R&B band, but not to my area. Until now.

A few months ago he told me his group was booked this week in my part of the country — but 400 miles away. Then a few weeks ago I heard on the radio that they were playing an hour away from me on the same tour so I emailed him to suggest getting together when he was near my town.

Somehow the wires got crossed. He texted me last Thursday: "I'm here." When I replied, "Where?" he said, "At (an airport 400 miles away). Call you from my hotel." An hour later, another text, "Where are you?" I said, "I'm at home." "Why aren't you here?" "Because you're 400 miles away!"

The phone rang. He sounded confused. "What do

you mean 400 miles away?" "That's where I live." "No! I thought you lived here." "Nope, I've always lived in this city." "I'm confused." "Clearly!"

"I got you a ticket to tomorrow's show here."

"Well, I'm sorry, but I can't get there tomorrow. I thought you'd get me a ticket for Saturday's show near me, which is what I said in my email."

"I blew it! I should have called you."

Yep. He should have called.

"I can't get you a ticket to the show near you, as all the comp tickets are taken by the other guys in the band."

Yep. He should have called.

"Bummer."

"Let me ask tomorrow to see if I can get one for you. I'll call you tomorrow before noon."

"Great. I'd love to see you in action."

Friday at 11:58 I got this text: "It might be possible." I took that to mean he had a line on a ticket and would let me know. I was hoping he'd succeed and was looking forward to meeting him and seeing the show. At 4:00 I got another text: "I'm getting dressed [for tonight's

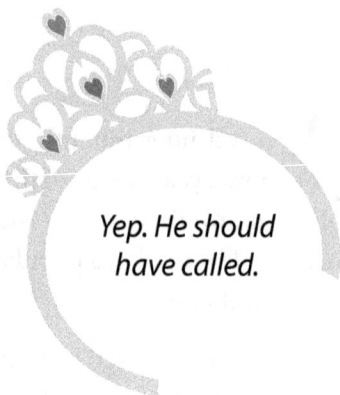

show]. I'll call you at 9:00."

Nine o'clock came and went. Nothing.

I thought, "Maybe their set went long. Or they all went out to dinner afterward," trying to give him some grace.

Saturday morning, nothing. Noon, nothing. Afternoon, nothing. I went out to dinner with a gal pal.

Sunday, nothing.

I scratch my head. I didn't berate him for his mistake. Was he too embarrassed to call? I could have lived with, "I'm so sorry. I blew it and I can't score a ticket for you. Let's explore what would work for us to meet up."

And this isn't a case of chalking it up to musicians being flaky. His day job is a responsible position!

Or is it just one more example of a way a man says he's not that into me? Pretty odd, I think, for a middle-aged man to behave this way. But I've seen it before so I shouldn't be surprised.

Does he know how to close?

I love dating men with a sales background.

Why?

Because they know how to close. How to ask for the order. How to pursue. How to keep clients happy.

"Close" in dating means to ask for your email address, phone number or date. I've found a lot of men don't know how to advance the relationship. Some are way too timid, taking weeks to ask for my number. Some are way too forward, asking for my number after one email exchange.

I understand many men don't like to exchange a lot of emails. They are either poor typists or poor spellers and feel it takes too long time to say what would take seconds on the phone. But I like to have a few email exchanges to get a sense of a man's ability to communicate clearly in writing and that he doesn't get sexual too soon.

Some men seem happy to have a pen pal relationship, stretching the emails out over weeks. This gets wearisome, too. Some men think it gentlemanly to wait until the woman is comfortable enough to offer her number. Other men offer theirs first,

> *Some men seem happy to have a pen pal relationship,*

knowing some women are not comfortable giving out her number. I prefer a man call me as it shows he has enough interest to pick up the phone. Giving me his number puts the onus on me.

Some women have no problem assertively asking, "When shall we get together?" I don't like to ask that as I feel a man needs to be assertive enough to ask for the "order" — a date. I don't want to be the one initiating, at least not at first. I don't mind initiating once we've gone out a few times.

In writing my book on sales, I discovered a common complaint from customers was salespeople who never asked for the order. Salespeople could have an hour-long meeting with the prospect uncovering their needs and constraints, then just thank the prospect at the end, without ever asking for the order. The prospect didn't feel it was their job to say, "It sounds like you have exactly what I need. How can I order?" They wanted the salesperson to ask for the business.

This is true in dating. If a woman has to prod a man to "ask for the order," he's probably not that interested or confident enough.

Salesmen also understand that if they want to secure the "account" (you) they have to make some effort to earn the "business" (your affection). They know they can't ignore a customer and expect to be received with open arms when they next connect. The customer may have found another supplier (man) to give them what they want. Good salesmen know if you want to keep a customer, you have to give them some attention.

These are basics that every salesperson knows. It would seem common sense, but to those outside of sales it doesn't appear to be common knowledge — or at least common practice.

The downside of dating salesmen is sometimes they are focused on putting up the numbers — closing the initial deal. If they are used to one-time sales, not ongoing orders, they don't fully understand the importance of "customer maintenance" — keeping you engaged beyond the initial conquest.

What do you think of dating men with a sales background? What do they do that works and doesn't work?

The tingle of possibility

Saturday, the first day of my professional association's conference this weekend, a married gal pal introduced me to a colleague of hers. He was tall and good looking. We only said hello as we scurried to our sessions.

I had reserved a table for 10 for Tuesday night's gala and invited her to be my guest. She said she'd promised to sit with him since he didn't know many people. I said to bring him along, as I had a well-positioned table and other fun guests.

He stopped me Sunday to thank me for inviting him to my table. He told me his name again and I said, "No need to reintroduce yourself. I always remember handsome men's names." He said, "I'll have to hang out with you more." We laughed and parted.

At the gala dinner he looked particularly smashing in his tux. But he was sitting two people away from me so I couldn't really chat with him. I did get a sense of his class and depth in our full-table discussions — and learned he was unattached. I wanted to get to know him more, so devised a system that wouldn't make it quite so blatant.

Since I'd assigned the seats alternating men and women, after the entree was cleared, I announced we would be doing a "man swap." Everyone looked at me quizzically. I said, "For us to get to know more people, each gentleman will take his napkin and water glass and move four seats to his left so he has a new woman on each side." They were delighted.

I'm afraid I nearly ignored the man on my right, as Mr. Handsome was on my left. We chatted and laughed easily. But all too soon the entertainment began. We whispered comments throughout and had a good time.

We'll see what evolves. He didn't ask for my card but he knows how to find me in the association directory. My friend said he told her the next day how much he enjoyed meeting me. If he doesn't make any further contact, oh well. I got to spend some time enjoying a handsome, articulate, intelligent, funny man's company. If he does follow up, we'll see where it goes.

The first post-divorce dance

I would never have guessed that one of the most difficult rites of passage after divorce was a first dance with a new man.

If you're like me, you may have slow danced with very few men other than your husband during your marriage (assuming he danced at all), unless you took dancing lessons that encouraged partner swapping. When I danced with another man it was typically a fast dance where we could do our own thing.

About a year after my divorce, a group of colleagues decided to go country western dancing. I love dancing so enthusiastically accepted the invitation.

One man took many of the gals in his van, with a few other guys saying they'd join us in a little while. After we got settled at a table, the gals began taking turns dancing with our one lone guy.

My turn on the floor with him was to a country two-step, with which I had but minimal familiarity. I felt stiff and awkward, even though my pal tried to lead me. He kept telling me to relax which did the opposite, triggering my feelings of ineptness and wondering if I was missing the "following" gene.

Struggling to stay in step, I was near tears when the song was thankfully over. I wondered why I was so emotional when my friend was just trying to help me have fun.

I realized part of the emotion was my missing the hand-in-glove comfort one feels when having had the same dance partner for decades. You know what to expect. You know his moves. You can relax and just feel the music and the connection to each other.

So I not only felt incompetent, I felt the loss of my companion of 20 years.

Often it's small things that trigger sadness and loss of the good things from a relationship. And those triggers can be present for years — decades for some people. So if you find yourself getting emotional over something like a dance, don't blame your partner or yourself. Just be willing to stay with the emotion and look at the core cause.

Sometimes I still feel I'm not the greatest follower. But I work to stay present to what's going on in the moment and enjoy whatever happens — even if his or my toes get a little mashed along the way.

What have you found to be difficult newly single firsts?

The triple-emotional-whammy wedding

Do you get emotional at weddings? Enveloped in the flood of love, joy and hope it is hard not to be. You are caught up in the palpable adoration between the happy couple. Maybe the nuptials remind you of how elated you felt at your wedding(s), immersed in the endorphins from being in love. Or perhaps the proceedings evoke memories of the grief you felt at the eventual loss of your love.

I haven't been to a wedding in the six years since my marriage dissolved, so I'm not sure what I'll feel at one I'll attend in a few weeks. In the past, I've become emotional because of the strong feelings of love that are typically present.

So my first emotional whammy is that I'll be at a wedding, period. I have no idea if I'll be overwhelmed by the joy and hope of the betrothed and their families. I'm hoping I won't be triggered by the fact that my own romantic fantasies of forever love went unrealized.

The second emotional whammy is that I've known the young groom since he was a baby. His parents, my ex and I were close friends. They live a few blocks away and it was common for one of us to drop in or borrow something regularly. Their family and my ex carpooled weekly to the same church. We often had dinner at each other's homes. We went on vacation together several times. I saw this young man and his brother grow up, shared in their celebrations and their troubling times. We hired them for yard work when they wanted spending money. The boys were like nephews and I have great fondness toward the groom and his brother. It will be emotional for me to see this young man enter this rite of passage to marry his long-time love.

And the third whammy is just a bit too surreal. My ex will officiate the ceremony. He is legally licensed to do so, although he never completed his ordination. This will be the first time I've seen him in five years. Will it be difficult to hear him talk about the sanctity of marriage, knowing that he didn't hold himself to that standard? Or the vow of commitment, knowing he violated that one too? I am over him and not bitter, but will it be difficult to hear him speak of values that I know he, himself, didn't act on? The hostess has said he will be

The third whammy is just a bit too surreal.

seated at my table, along with a few other friends who know each other, as none of us know anyone else at the reception.

To do my utmost to take care of myself, I have invited a dear and doting friend to be my date. He has been apprised of my probable emotionality and that I will, no doubt, need to lean on him. He has enthusiastically agreed to take on this task. Plus he dresses up really well and is a great dancer!

While I usually consider myself a strong woman, I think it helps to know when you may be especially vulnerable and pre-plan ways to make sure you are taken care of. And with this triple whammy wedding, I will need all the support I can muster!

Are you emotional at weddings or other events? If so, how do you take care of yourself?

99 men on the wall

Maybe the little ditty "99 men on the wall" will replace the old song we sang loudly on long bus/car drives, but only women will be singing it.

Today I have a meet/date with man number 99. It's taken nearly 5 years to go out with 99 men and I have slowed down a lot in the last 2 years. No longer do I feel like the kid in Baskin-Robbins wanting to taste all the flavors. I have now narrowed down the flavors that interest me and can often tell beforehand if a man has qualities that appeal to me or not. Most often not.

I continue to be open to new encounters, but am more discerning if a man telegraphs "We don't have the same values" even before meeting. I can often tell that by the content of his emails and phone conversation, by what he chooses to talk about, the questions he asks me (or doesn't), how much he shares the conversation.

If you were looking for a dream job or fabulous house, you might investigate 100 before finding the one that meets most of your needs. Dating nearly 100 men isn't the goal — finding a great match is.

When I share my dating numbers with interested

friends, most gasp, "I haven't dated 99 people in my whole life." It seems few have, unless they were very active in their high school and/or college years. Most people have dated from zero to several dozen people. Then they met their mate or withdrew to either no or infrequent dating. I am an anomaly.

People say, "I wouldn't have the patience for that," or "I don't have the time," or "I'd just give up." Yes, there are considerations for staying active in the dating pool. There can be times of furious activity (like when I had seven dates with six guys in five days) and long stretches of treading water. There are the days of hopefulness when you've met someone with whom you think you're a match, then disappointment when he stops calling with no explanation or you decide he isn't who you thought him to be.

One weighs the options for staying in the emotional whirlpool. You can just drift down the dating river, hoping to bump into your soul mate. You can swim upstream in the rapids, trying to attain someone who isn't interested, getting frustrated and bitter along the way. Or you can tread water until you connect with a possible match, then both swim in the dating pool together,

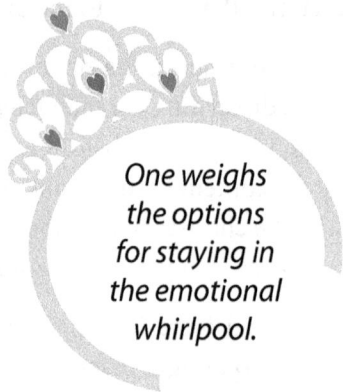

> *One weighs the options for staying in the emotional whirlpool.*

playing and interacting to see if you like each other.

Giving up is an option, of course, but I have learned much about what I want (and don't want), as well as about men in general, I do not see that as the best option. And I've gained several dozen men-pal treasures for whom I'm continually grateful.

So going out with 99 men may sound daunting. But it's better than the option — to be lonely and bitter. I'm staying in the pool until I find my guy — or he finds me.

Where are the men like us?

My 55-year-old successful gal pal was recounting her 5-year dating experience. She bemoaned her encounters with men who were not comparable economically or emotionally. It is a common lament for successful midlife women. The wail is, "Where are the men like us?" We shared our various successes and frustrations with finding available men organically and online dating. We agreed it was pretty easy to get a date with someone online.

The challenge is to get a date with someone with whom we want a second date and who feels the same. Most often, neither of you wants a second date. Sometimes you wouldn't mind seeing him again, but he doesn't feel the same. Or he'd like to see you again, but you're clear there's no appeal for you.

My friend said she'd begun to explore It's Just Lunch and Dinner for Six, but wasn't willing to pay $5000 for 10 dates — $500/date seemed extreme. When she queried the sales rep for one of these on how many over-50 men were enrolled in her area, the rep wouldn't say. She was told there were 200 local men members, and she did the math. If 100 of them were over 50, how many of them might be a reasonable match? She decided she wasn't willing to pay such a large fee for the miniscule chance one of these 100 men would be compatible with her.

She's tried hanging out in upscale bars and had men approach her. But none resulted in a date.

Dating her clients isn't a possibility. She can try to date friends of friends and find possible dates through chance encounters doing errands or hobbies. She was considering attending over-50 singles events, but she's shy so would feel more comfortable doing this with a pal. She'll also try taking classes that may draw men at her level, and attending some more professional events.

I'm told educated, accomplished women of all ages face this situation. If a man is as well educated or ac-complished as she is, he has other deal breakers. Are we pickier than other women? Perhaps. We don't want to settle for someone who doesn't meet basic standards. Yes, there are plenty of good men who may not make as much money as an accomplished woman, or who may not be as educated. For some women, that's not a prob-lem. But for some, it is.

How have you met available men of equal station in life as you? How have you dealt with a wide disparity between your accomplishments and men you've dated? If it hasn't been a problem, how did you make peace with the differences?

10 Tips for Successful Dating Over 40

Y ou've been single for a while. You would like to have a special man in your life. But how?

Women reentering the dating scene after a long absence need to first examine if they are ready to date again. After all, not only is there the possibility of being swept off your feet by a romantic, loving man, there's the chance of being swept over the cliff of heartbreak. Here are some tips on how to ensure you enjoy your adventure of dating after 40, not dread the next coffee date.

Examine your expectations Although you say you want a tall, dark, handsome, loving, articulate, successful man, very few of them look like George Clooney. Most have at least one of the following: receding hairline (if any hair at all), paunch, some "baggage" from past relationships, kids still needing some guidance and perhaps loans, and some less-than-stellar housekeeping habits. Know what you can live with and what are deal breakers. An occasional sock left on the floor is tolerable – his 35-year-old son living with Dad because he's waiting for his band's big break is not.

Have courage It takes courage to get your cute on to meet someone for a first coffee date. There's always the possibility he will leave after 10 minutes explaining he's just not attracted to you (as I had happen once). Ouch! But it says more about him than you. In my experience of going out with 101 men in five years (this was not a life goal!), about half of the first dates don't result in a second. So you have to have the courage to keep putting yourself out there if you are clear you want a special man in your life again.

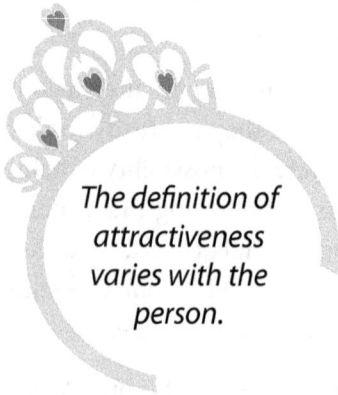

> *The definition of attractiveness varies with the person.*

Assess your assets If you have been out of the dating scene awhile, it's easy to think, "Who would possibly think I'm attractive?" The definition of attractiveness varies with the person. Some men find a dazzling smile trumps a few extra pounds. Others find long legs or a hour-glass figure outshine a few wrinkles. Discover your own assets. And dress to them. Get a makeover at a nearby department store. Tell the personal shopper you want some date clothes — and wear them! Sometimes it takes others to see assets that we mistakenly call liabilities.

Be willing to go on "practice dates." The first few dates with strangers are nerve-wracking. You're wondering, "How will I greet him?" "What if he leaves after a few minutes?" "What if he tries to kiss me?" "What if he's odious?" So go out with a few men who you aren't overwhelmingly attracted to but seem interesting. You'll have your wits about you more than if you are agog over someone. Keep the date short — ideally just coffee. You don't want to waste either of your time, but you may meet a nice guy.

Vet him before agreeing to even coffee. You can avoid many dud dates by talking to a potential suitor a few times on the phone before agreeing to even coffee. If you feel you've had enough practice dates and are only interested in meeting men with a potential future, then learn to hear cues he's worth meeting. Men disclose a lot by emails and on the phone. If he talks 90% of the time and doesn't ask you a question (or the question is, "What are you wearing?"), you know you don't need to meet. He doesn't know how to be in conversation — let alone relationship — with someone.

See every encounter as a possible treasure. Several dozen of the 101 men have remained pals — in some cases, treasured friends. I wouldn't have crossed paths with these men any other way except we were in the dating pool. So if you meet a lovely man and after a few dates just don't feel any romantic connection, you don't have to sever the relationship. You can ask if he'd be open to your being friends. Some will say yes, others no.

Be "in wonder" if he does something you think odd. Some behaviors may be just odd. An executive licked his knife at a white-table-clothed restaurant. Another professional ate his salad with his fingers. One emailed me that I was "the one" but he hadn't bothered to contact me in months. I often scratch my head, saying, "What is he thinking?" It's no surprise to you that men and women think and act differently. Expecting a man to act like you and your gal pals is setting yourself up for disaster. So instead of being judgmental, try to be curious and "in wonder." Think, "Let me imagine a scenario where this would be considered appropriate." Of course, if you are wondering that too often, probably time to let this one go.

If he's not a jerk, agree to another encounter. First dates don't often end with you both enamored with the other. But love can grow if you give it a little time. So if he wasn't a jerk, odious, or had other deal breakers, agree to another encounter if he asks. But make sure it's reasonably short – a walk, museum visit, lunch or dinner. I've congratulated myself when a man wanted a second date that would have taken all day and I would have felt trapped, yet I insisted on something shorter. In a second date, one lets their hair down a bit more, so deal-breaker behaviors or information come out ("I still live with my wife/mother").

Beware of falling too fast If you've been without a partner for a while, it's easy to fall for the first nice, attentive guy who comes along. Resist, as his niceness may have nothing to do with his interest in you, but just how he behaves with every woman. He was taught chivalry, which is endearing, but it doesn't necessarily mean he's showing you that he thinks you're special. Loneliness causes us to misinterpret politeness for attraction. Keep your heart in check until enough time has passed that he's shown his caring for you multiple times.

Keep the attitude of adventure. Just like a treasure hunt, you never know when or where you'll uncover a prized gem. It's easy to get discouraged (after 101 men!), but know that you are learning a lot about yourself, men, and what you want along the way. Just like an explorer, you'll find lots of dead ends. But if you are committed to your goal of finding a special sweetie, you can't give up. And you'll be amazed at how having an adventuresome spirit is alluring to many men!

The experiment

I'm an equal-opportunity dater. I've gone out with Caucasian, Black, Latino, Asian, Indian, Native American and mixed-race men. Although it doesn't always come up, I know some have been Christian, Jewish, Muslim, Buddhist, Hindu, agnostic and atheist. None of these on their own are deal makers or deal breakers. My interest or disinterest depends on many other elements.

So it surprised me when some Black men asked me if they are an "experiment." If going out with them was part of satisfying some curiosity of mine. The first time I was asked this I was confused, so probed.

"What do you mean by 'experiment?'"

"Some women have heard about certain characteristics that Black men supposedly possess and they want to see if it's true."

I almost fell out of my chair.

These "characteristics" could really be described as physical "attributes." And the Black men got tired of being with women who just wanted to see for themselves, without any interest in a relationship. They'd spent time and energy getting to know a woman and then after a roll or two in the hay, she'd had her curiosity satisfied (and perhaps other things as well) and was on her way. She really wasn't interested in anything beyond confirming (or not) the rumors she'd heard.

No one likes to feel like a curiosity, something to be examined and then tossed aside. We want to invest time with people who have an interest in the whole package, not just a single part. So I understood these men's skepticism and caution.

No one likes to feel like a curiosity,

Men I had no interest in have asked if they could fondle certain body parts. How could they possibly think that I'd say yes? They were curious, and no doubt, felt there was no harm in asking as they got the message I wouldn't be seeing them again.

Have you ever felt that someone was with you just to have his curiosity quenched? What happened?

Lucy, the football and dating

When you think of Peanuts' Lucy and the football, you see a comic strip series where Charlie Brown, the ever hopeful and trusting soul, believes Lucy when she tells him — once again — that she'll hold the ball for him to kick. Every time — for decades — she pulls the ball away at the last minute, causing Charlie to land hard on his backside. No matter how much she's promised him she won't, she does.

In dating, I'm surprised by how many men think it's perfectly okay to pull out the football in many ways. It can be as simple as he says he'll call on a certain day and he doesn't. While you might not sit by the phone waiting (as you may have when younger), if you have any connection with him you look forward to the call.

But it doesn't come. He may (or may not) text or call later, saying he got tied up. This may (or may not) be accompanied by an apology.

Or he tells you he'll meet you at 7:00 and 7:15 comes

and goes with no notification of his lateness. He may appear (or not) and explain it away (or not). He may apologize, but often there is no mention of his tardiness, let alone an apology.

Perhaps he suggests hanging out together this Saturday. He says he'll call you Saturday morning to confirm. When you don't hear from him by noon, you call him so you can determine your afternoon's schedule. "Oh," he tells you, "a friend called and we're going motorcycle riding for the day."

Yes, all these examples are of rude, thoughtless, self-centered behaviors. But can so many men be so inconsiderate?

Can so many men be so inconsiderate?

A male pal explained that when a man says, "I'll talk to you tomorrow" he's not so much making a commitment, but more expressing a possibility. I, and many of the people with whom I pal around, believe your word is your bond. You don't say you're going to do something and then not do it unless you communicate and renegotiate with the person to whom you've committed.

I know in today's society this is a rarity.

For those of us who expect someone to follow through with what they say, we behave as if the promise

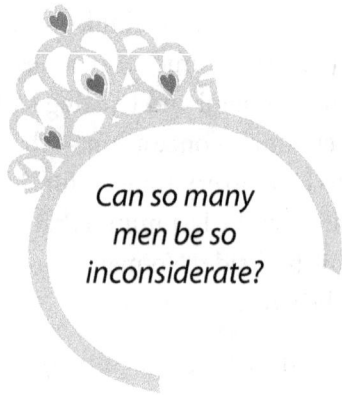

will come through. So if a man invites me to dinner, I'll determine what I'm going to wear and make sure it's clean and pressed. I'll plan my chores to make sure I have the evening free with no pressing duties to distract me. I'll wash and curl or straighten my hair so it looks and smells good. While not obsessing, I imagine how much fun it is to be with him and perhaps think of some topics I want to share.

Then, boom, the call half-hour before I'm to leave, telling me he's tied up and has to reschedule. The football was pulled out just as I was beginning to kick it.

While we can all occasionally have unexpected situations occur that make us need to reschedule our social calendar, if it happens more than once in a short time, I see it as his 1) lack of respect for me, 2) inability to manage his life, 3) belief that this is an okay way to treat people and/or 4) absence of real interest in me.

I've let men with whom I've been smitten pull the ball out numerous times. I gave them too much grace. And it hurt more than my tush. Now, I look for the signs much more quickly. If, on the second occurrence I state my displeasure and he responds that I should be more flexible or spontaneous, I know that hc and I have very different values.

Then I take my football to play with someone who respects the players and follows the same rules of good sportsmanship.

Managing
expectations

On our first date, as we walked to his car, he said, "I'll open the door for you, but don't get used to this."

I asked why.

"Because I don't usually open the door for women. In six months, I will have stopped and you'll think something is wrong. Nothing's wrong. It's just not my habit to open the door for a woman. And I'm too old to develop new habits."

"I know from our conversations that you are a man who strives for personal continuous improvement. So if you were really into a woman and your opening the door for her was important to her, I bet you'd work to make that a habit."

"That's true" he admitted. "But I've learned not to over promise on things that just aren't in my nature to keep up over time. It creates expectations that I'm not likely to meet. And that creates disappointment."

"That makes sense. You don't want to pretend to be someone you're not."

"Exactly. For example, I've learned to give only a 10-minute massage. I used to give an hour, but then the woman would expect an hour's massage each time. I can do 10 minutes frequently, but I can't do an hour."

I appreciated his candor, even though I also appreciate chivalry. It made me wonder about what each of us does early on in a relationship that is for show — to ingratiate ourselves to the other. I looked back on my own behaviors to see how I can be different in the early stages of a relationship than after we've been together a while.

In all honesty, I think I've been nicer in the early stages, not saying when something bothered me. I don't know if it was insecurity that the guy might not like me, or just feeling that it wasn't polite to say something. Now I'm more confident and more assertive. I don't put up with the BS I used to.

What have you observed yourself doing — or not doing — that you changed as you got to know someone? Have you purposefully learned to not try to be someone you're not when you know you'll revert to your true self in short order? Have you experienced someone who put on behaviors at first, but then dropped them as you got to know each other?

The fix-up

Weeks ago my friend mentioned his brother was coming into town for a few days to celebrate my friend's birthday. My pal said he'd like his brother to meet me. "You'll like him" he declared. Since I like my pal a lot, I thought if his brother is like him, yes I would enjoy that.

The weeks passed without further mention of this -- no invitation to join them on any outing; no set time to rendezvous.

A few evenings ago, I heard my friend's familiar doorbell ring pattern beckoning me to answer. There he was, with said brother, saying they'd just gone to the market and did I want to come over for dinner. Normally, I'd jump at an offer for someone else's cooking, but I'd just taken my week's dinners off the grill. Since I had abundance, I offered for them to join me for dinner.

The brother was shorter than me, lived an 8-hour drive away and immediately began calling me "Sweetie," something I deplore as a sooner-than-earned privilege. I endured his turning the conversation back to himself throughout dinner, and in the course of the discussion, learned he was single. They invited me to join them the next day, along with my friend's girlfriend, for the birthday dinner, saying how much fun I'd have and how they'd love to have me there.

Now the brother's occasional flirts began to make sense! My friend was trying to fix us up!

It felt like in college, coupled friends suggested I go along with them and a guy friend of theirs to an outing. It wasn't as if they thought we'd be a good match; just someone to entertain their pal so they wouldn't feel awkward being a couple with him. Rarely did these events go well. Generally, they were excruciating. I put up with someone either too shy to be engaging, clearly disinterested in getting to know me despite my trys to start conversations, or too aggressively horny to keep his hands to himself.

So I declined the brother's invitation for the next day. I wondered if I was being selfish to not want to share in my friend's birthday activities. But then I thought, if it were important to him for me to be there, he would have asked beforehand.

Dry spells

There are lulls in dating life when you have no active prospects. You've moved to the "friends" category anyone who's contacted you in the past. No one interesting has appeared on the horizon.

For most daters, this is their most frequent experience, lingering, perhaps checking online sites for new arrivals. But either no one contacts us or returns our emails.

So we cool our jets, not giving up our desire to have someone special in our lives, but feeling we've done everything we're willing to do for the time being. We know there are other activities in which we could engage if we were being aggressive in our search. But right now, singles dances and matchmakers feel like more work than we'd like.

We try to not drop into a defeatist mentality, succumbing to the oft-chanted mantra of others whose cynicism has taken over: "The good ones are all taken or gay," "The only ones left in the dating pool are losers" (which, by definition, means we must be in that category since we're still available).

If you find yourself in a lull, buck up. Enjoy your opportunity to be self-focused (or as much as you can if you have kids at home). You get to do whatever you want, without concerning yourself with anyone else's feelings or desires. You get to eat in bed, wear your ratty night clothes, not shave your legs — if you want.

However, don't let your self-absorbed habits become too en-grained. Be mindful that you will want to repair your slovenliness once you have someone else in your life.

Don't let your self-absorbed habits become too engrained.

But for now, enjoy. Get to know yourself even better. Find out what you really like to do. See this time as a chance to spread your wings, un-encumbered with concern for a partner.

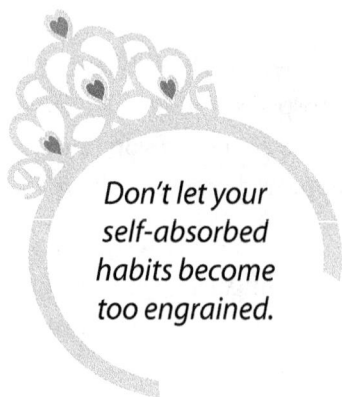

Setting boundaries vs. playing games

No one likes it when someone they are dating "plays games," which is a nebulous description of someone trying to manipulate the other. (We're not talking Monopoly, Bridge, or tennis here!) But very few people can articulate what constitutes a game. (However, it is commonly agreed that if an "attached," [e.g., non-single] person acts as if they are unattached, s/he is "playing games." Or if when asked "are you seeing someone else?" they respond, "no," meaning "not at this very exact moment as I'm with you and she's at home.")

Some people consider arbitrary rules to be game playing. For example, women who won't call men under any circumstance, or pay for a meal, or have an x-dates-before-sex criteria.

So when does setting boundaries cross the line to becoming a game? For example, although I understand why men offer me their phone number before I offer mine, I prefer to have him make the first move. So I respond with my number and invite him to call. My experience is that if I give him my number and he doesn't call, he's not that interested or doesn't have the initiative I'm looking for. If I call him first, I never get a sense for either of these.

I also don't like to be on the phone after 10:00 especially for the first few calls. For example, an initial call from a new man came in at 7:30 p.m. No problem. We chatted for 30 minutes, then he said he needed to do a quick errand and would call back absolutely no later than 9:00. No problem.

So when his call came in at 10:00, I sent it directly to voice mail. Could I have answered? Sure. But, 1) he was an hour later than he'd promised, which is not a good sign and 2) 10:00 on a work night is too late unless one knows the other is a night owl or has an already established relationship. If I'd answered, I'd be sending the signal that he doesn't have to honor his promises and I'll accept his calls whenever he dials. Nope. Not going there.

> *I'd be sending the signal that he doesn't have to honor his promises*

Is that playing games? Some would consider it so. Others would say I was setting a boundary of honoring my own needs first. Is this selfish? I don't think so. If you bend your boundaries at the beginning of a relationship, a man will never learn to honor the ones that are important to you.

Does this mean you should be rigid? Not necessarily. But I've found when I waive my own boundaries, I'm in for a heap of trouble. He never believes any of my stated boundaries because I didn't stand up for them (and for what I wanted/needed).

So what do you think is a "game" vs. a boundary? Have you ever purposefully played games in midlife dating? What did you do and why? What boundaries have you bent and what were the results? What haven't you waived and are glad you didn't?

How soon is too soon?

General wisdom is to take some time to be alone after any relationship ends.

The shorter the time in the relationship, the less time it takes to recover. I once heard that most people need 25%-50% of a relationship's duration before being ready to have another relationship.

After talking for two weeks, a man disclosed that the reason he listed himself on a dating site is that his partner of 7 years died — two months ago.

My first reaction was, whoa — that's way too soon to be dating. But in discussing his situation he seemed very grounded about it. And since grieving is unique to every person, it wasn't up to me to decide what was right or proper for him.

That's way too soon to be dating

He said her sudden death made him realize that life is short, not to take anything for granted, and that he didn't want to languish in self-pity. He had honored her every day of their relationship so he doesn't think dating now is in any way dishonoring her. She'd want him to move on in his life and be happy.

However, he knew he was currently not looking for a replacement relationship. He'd like companionship and someone to enjoy.

Generally, I'd shy away from pursuing anything with anyone in this situation as I wouldn't want to be a rebound sweetie. That usually means heartache.

Deafening silence

An interesting man contacts you through a dating site, but he lives several states away. Even with the distance, you decide he's intriguing enough to get to know. Besides, you're going to be in his general area in two weeks, and perhaps he'd consider driving to meet you.

You get to know each other via email and phone, talking every few days. The calls are punctuated by frequent laughter. Your emails show caring and interest in each other's lives. He isn't daunted by the 2-hour drive to take you to dinner and a jazz club when you're in his area.

He says he's nervous to meet you, which you find sweet, yet odd for a confident, accomplished man.

A big grin brightens his face when he meets you and the evening is a fun ebb and flow of sharing personal experiences, philosophies, and laughter. Flirty arm touching and hand holding evolve naturally.

He even whisks you to the dance floor for a romantic slow song, but you are the one who is nervous now because he performs at ballroom dancing exhibitions. He holds you close, cheek-to-cheek, and you sort of freeze, losing any hint of rhythm. He even resorts to counting the beat in your ear — how humiliating! What happened? You're usually a reasonably good dancer, although not accomplished at ballroom. But he wasn't asking you to fox trot, samba or waltz — this was just a simple sway-step! But you found the sudden intimacy too much sensory overload.

He seems to overlook your dancing melt down as you return to your table and listen to the rest of the set.

In the car back to your hotel, he asks if you had a good time. "Absolutely!" you respond enthusiastically. "Great company, good music, fun laughter, good food." He pulls you to him for a brief kiss.

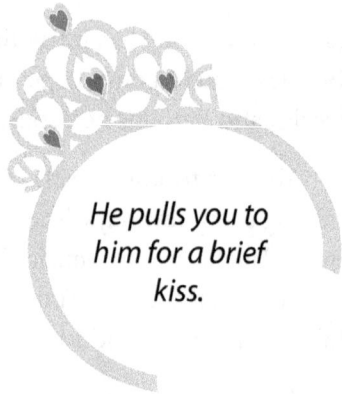

He pulls you to him for a brief kiss.

You thank him for making the long drive. In a joking way he says he should take a nap before returning home, asking if you have a couch in your room. "No," you lie, "But there's one in the hotel lobby. I'm sure we could get you a blanket," you continue in a joking tone of voice. If he's serious, you're clear you're not going to have a man you just met come to your hotel room.

"Well, you will invite me to your room, won't you?" he asks. "I bet they have rooms available if you're too tired to drive home," you respond, now incredulous that he thinks you would have him up to your room the first time you met. Was that his expectation — that you'd have sex on the first date?

He drives to the hotel front door. You expect he'll turn off the car and get out to hug you goodbye. Instead, he keeps the motor running and doesn't unhook his seat belt. You thank him again, lean over and give him a quick kiss. Then you open your door and enter the hotel.

Back in your room, you email him a sincere thank you, saying you enjoyed your time together. Days pass and nothing from him. He usually responds within hours to your emails. The silence is deafening.

WTF??? Was the dancing incident too much? Or not inviting him up to your hotel room? Or did he realize that the geographical distance was too much?

We women drive ourselves crazy trying to figure out what happened when a man disappears. We have to come to grips with the fact that if a man wants to stay connected to you, he will. If he's not interested, he won't. It is so simple, yet we make it hard — at least hard on ourselves.

We need to just enjoy the good times when we're having them and if we never hear from him again, oh well! His loss. Not worth our worrying and fretting over. Move on. He's obviously not your "One" if he doesn't make contact. Keep looking. And have fun while you are.

"I don't know if my equipment still works!"

While munching sushi and margaritas, the sweet, 62-year-old widower shared his concern as we discussed dating. His wife of 3 decades had died 18 months ago and he was dipping into the dating pool.

What he found was a lot of aggressive, sexually hungry women. He was dumfounded that they tried to seduce him on the first date. He was not happy about this.

One woman invited him to her house for their first date. When he arrived, she'd laid out various battery-operated toys for him to choose. He was stunned. Not completely understanding what was expected from him, he allowed her to explain each one before he hightailed it home.

"Is this what women expect now? A roll in the hay on the first date? I haven't been intimate with a woman in a while. I don't even know if my equipment still works!"

I felt sorry for the dear man. This was only one of a number of encounters where women tried to seduce him on the first encounter. "I need to feel something for a woman before I jump into bed with her. I've never been into casual sex. If this is the expectation, I'm not cut out for this."

On one hand, I was sad that he had to encounter such uncouth women. On the other hand, I was glad to hear it wasn't just women who encountered inappropriate, lecherous people in the dating pool.

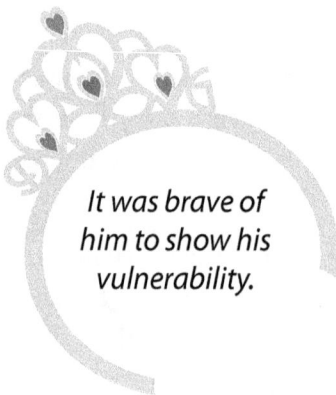

Also, I thought it was brave of him to show his vulnerability to me exposing his uncertainty about sex. It was a refreshing change from the many men who boasted of their sexual prowess, often even before we met.

It was brave of him to show his vulnerability.

I assured him that there are many classy women who also want to wait until they have an emotional connection before getting intimate. I told him he will learn to weed out the inappropriate ones through more probing on the phone so he'll improve his ratio of appropriate to inappropriate meetings. I shared that I am still not perfect at that vetting, but I am much, much better than in the beginning.

For those who've not dated in decades, the modern dating scene can be quite a shock. It is surprising what people tell or ask you, sometimes before you've even met. The assumptions and behaviors of some can be abhorrent. You can get scared and angry. Or you can realize that your assumptions that people are thoughtful, classy and appropriate are too generous, based on your own circle of friends.

However, there are good, honest, thoughtful, generous people in the dating pool. We just have to hone our skills to find them.

Two-step for one

Yee-haw!

Country Western dancing. Let's go!

This was my feeling as I decided to try something new, a bit out of my comfort zone, in my quest to experiment with meeting available men in the "natural" way. Common advice from dating experts is to take a class in something that interests you. So I thought I'd give it a try.

Since I know no Country Western dances, my gal pal — also known as my courage crutch — and I knew we needed to show up for the lessons an hour before the club's normal hours.

When we arrived, a line-dance lesson was in full swing. We hopped right in. Although the instructor wasn't as thorough as my Jazzercise instructor, I followed along reasonably well, messing up less and less as the lesson progressed. My gal pal, however, bailed about half way through and sat down.

Our problem began when the next dance was a couples two-step. All those interested in learning gathered on the dance floor. The men picked a partner. Just like in high school, no one picked either of us. Feeling a bit rejected, we sat down rather than two-step alone. We watched in interest as the lesson progressed, sure we could have picked up the reasonably simple steps.

The lesson over, open dancing began. We realized we were like new-born calves in a sea of mature cows and bulls. Nearly all the dancers knew the intricate patterns to the music. We realized we'd look like innocent rodeo lambs released from the gate, with only a few seconds before we were writhing under a cowboy's powerful ropes, squealing forlornly. We didn't want feign we knew what we were doing — although admittedly we were used to doing that since we were both consultants.

So we settled for marveling at the smooth, energetic moves of the elderly man twirling several 20-something girls. We were enthralled by the several dozen various-shaped bodies all moving to their own style. And we stealthily hid from any potential partner's gaze as the single men hunted for available women. We knew we were not ready to be hauled around the dance floor by someone who actually knew what he was doing.

At the band's first break, we decided it was time for us to head back to our barns. We could be satisfied that we'd tried a new pasture and we'd survived with our dignities in tact.

Following a man's lead

Since my divorce, I've had a fear of dance classes. Not because I'm concerned about following the steps — I'm reasonably adept at that. But it's for another reason — something that I think might plague other accomplished women.

It might be something that you struggle with yourself.

I'm concerned that I won't be able to follow a man's lead.

For 20 years, I slow-danced with one man — my husband. I knew his moves. He wasn't a strong leader (in anything, really), but I learned his steps and could follow along quite nicely.

Post divorce, I slow-danced with only a few beaus, and rarely in public. They held me so closely, it was impossible not to sway with them.

But dance class — in the arms of a strange man, doing a dance with specific steps I was supposed to follow. Oy vey! It was so scary, I stayed away from any dancing that would require being in a hold.

This was magnified exponentially when I had the melt down on the dance floor with the astronaut a few months ago. When this man I had just met pulled me close on our first (and only) dance, I froze. I didn't move when he tried to move me. My statue-like state caused him to count the beat in my ear. I was humiliated.

So a few weeks ago I decided I needed to break through this barrier. I screwed up my courage and attended a salsa dance class, having convinced a gal pal to accompany me for moral support.

I screwed up my courage

The instructor had the women rotate partners, so I danced with 8 men several times. Most of them were weak leads, but I fought the urge to take over. I survived — and even enjoyed it. But how would I be with a man who knew how to lead? Would I be able to follow even when they weren't leading? Passivity wasn't a strong suit.

This weekend, I got to experiment again, attending the second class. This time, there were only 3 students — all women — so we got to take turns dancing with

the three instructors.

Commenting on what I thought was a normal hand hold in our first turn together, the primary instructor, Frank, said, "I'd hate to meet you in a back alley — you're strong." It didn't seem like a compliment. In our second turn, I thought I was following nicely when he said "You have to let the man lead. If you don't, he feels emasculated." I wasn't appreciating his editorializing. Just tell me what I need to do to dance well, don't lecture to me.

It fed into my insecurities about not knowing how to follow. So much so, I checked out the impressions with a younger, strong-leading instructor with whom I'd danced. He said I followed just fine.

What's your experience with learning to follow? Do you have any issues with it or do you just naturally follow a man's dance lead? Have you gained any insights if you had to learn this behavior?

When your net worth is bigger than his

Bev asks:

"How does a woman over 50 whose divorce settlement made her a millionaire + handle dating when most men will not have anywhere near her net worth?"

First, since divorces can be devastating financially for both parties, it's great you came out with a nice sum.

And it's true that many people experienced financial setbacks following divorce, the recent down economy also created serious financial problems for even previously successful folks. So while not every potential suitor may have experienced financial losses, many will have.

So my first suggestion is to ward off opportunists by not letting on at all about your financial situation for many, many months into dating someone exclusively. While there are many, many good, honest, upstanding men in the dating pool, I've heard enough stories of scam artists to be cautious.

Take some extra precautions, like not wearing flashy jewelry, nor talking about expensive vacations or your high-end neighborhood. Look objectively at items or conversational topics that you think are common among your friends that would telegraph wealth. Then eliminate those from your first handful of dates with a man. Switch from your Coach purse to an off brand. Instead of St. John knits, wear something more pedestrian.

A well-off friend purposefully drives his Echo instead of his convertible Mercedes for the first few dates with a woman. If she comments on his crummy car he stops seeing her. He says he's found that his Mercedes attracts more gold diggers and he just doesn't want to waste his time.

You want a man who will fall for you, not your nest egg.

If it doesn't appear he has the resources to treat for dinners and experiences you enjoy, after some months you can offer to have him as your guest. But not at first. Let him pick the restaurant that is comfortable for his budget. You can have a lot of fun doing low-cost activities.

You have to decide at some point if you'd be happy with someone who can't afford the same lifestyle as you can, or if you'd be okay with paying his part to join you. Generally, mentally healthy men like to be able to provide or at least carry their own weight financially. It will usually gnaw on a man when he is continually financially unable to keep up with his woman and it can destroy the relationship.

The activity partner

When your friends are all coupled and rarely want to do something social without their spouse, it can be hard to find activity buddies. Sure, there are singles events in many locales, but often they feel like an audition instead of just having people with whom to do things. And other than your all being single, you may find you have little in common with these folks so make few connections.

Sometimes you come upon someone on a dating site who likes to do similar things as you, but you know there's no romantic interest. Other times the person will say clearly, "Looking for an activity partner." It takes the pressure off wondering if he'll try to kiss you in the middle of the first date!

"Looking for an activity partner."

I was contacted recently by someone who refreshingly said he was just looking for a pal with whom to do things. We like to do a lot of the same things, and I recognized him as a community leader from his pics. He shared that his wife of three decades died last year and he wanted someone to go to the movies and hikes and bike rides. Plus, he lives in my neighborhood!

So I will meet my new potential friend tomorrow for lunch and see if we like each other enough to want to do things together. Our phone conversation pointed to "yes" on the would-we-enjoy-hanging-out-together dial. And I don't think I'll have to be concerned about his trying to sneak a kiss on the first encounter.

Have you nurtured strangers to become activity partners? Have they ever transitioned to romantic partners?

Dipping into salsa

Salsa — a spicy dip and a spicy dance. My latest experience is with the latter.

Dr. Philling myself, I asked how online dating was working for me. I've met some interesting men and gathered a few sweethearts from the experience, but know there are other options. Yet, being situationally introverted, I'm not great about getting myself to in-person singles events.

Like many midlife daters, I want to maximize my ability to meet intriguing singles. So I've been pep-talking myself into more in-person activities. Doubting I'll meet anyone in my 99% all-women Jazzercise classes, I've expanded my reach — and my comfort zone.

So this weekend I convinced a gal pal to accompany me to a salsa dance class. Arriving 10 minutes before class time we were surprised we were the only ones there. "Cool," we muttered to each other, "abundant attention from the male instructor." Then three men swept in — we were surprised we were now in the minority.

Eventually, there were 8 couples including one other male instructor who patiently muttered the steps as each woman took turns in his arms. The instructor did a great job of having us change partners every few minutes so we got to practice not stepping on each other's toes with multiple novices.

The instructor, a mid-life, pot-bellied man with a comb over was surprisingly sensual when he got his hips going. If men knew how alluring a good dancer is, I think more would take up ballroom dancing.

Even though I had lessons many years ago, I knew it would be best to start from scratch. So when the instructor asked about our experience, I said to assume I knew nothing. I was then pleased when he singled me out to compliment my turns.

Did I meet anyone I thought I'd want to date? No. But I did feel comfortable in the environment which made me want to return. After a few more lessons, I'd feel comfortable attending one of their salsa dance parties and expanding my social circle.

The experience reminded me of the process of dating. At first it feels awkward and uncomfortable. But with a little guidance and practice, you feel more secure. Within a short amount of time, you're ready for more and looking forward to new experiences.

What have you tried that is like dating — you're timid at first but then quickly get comfortable?

Feeling powerless in dating

A lot of people are feeling powerless lately — about their job security, their financial future, their retirement. Those of us who are dating are used to feeling powerless.

Men say they feel powerless because women set the pace in dating. Women decide how quickly or slowly a relationship advances. A man can feel helpless to get a woman to return his calls or go out with him.

Women say they feel powerless because men control the pace. How many times have you heard women complain about waiting for a man to call? Nowadays, women call men, of course. But even with all the advancements women have made, many still feel some stigma in calling a man or asking him out.

Recently I received an email after a second date with a man I liked. He said he enjoyed our dinner and would call before he left for an international trip a few days later. He'd always kept his word in the months we'd been talking. But not this time. So the quandary is do I call or email him, or just wait for him to surface if/when he wants to connect. I made it clear I'd like to see him again on our date and in our last correspondence. But maybe he felt otherwise as his lack of communication could seem.

I think the best thing we can do to protect ourselves from a feeling of powerlessness is to keep busy. Fill up your life with activities you enjoy and dating others until you're getting what you need/ want in the relationship. If you are talking to and seeing others, you don't worry about not hearing from one — even if he is the one you like the best.

You don't want to come across as needy or a stalker

You don't want to come across as needy or a stalker by texting/IMing/emailing/calling him multiple times. Let him come to you. If you make it clear you would say yes to an invitation from him and he still doesn't move forward, that doesn't need to hold you back. Keep moving forward on your own path without waiting for him to come with you. There are plenty of men who would love to have your company so don't wait on one who isn't sure.

The low-speed chase

Y ou've heard of cops engaging in high-speed chases to catch criminals. Then OJ Simpson made the low-speed chase a new buzz word when he was avoiding arrest. The concept can be applied to dating, although it is not to avoid incarceration. It might be to avoid entanglement, but it also might be a sound strategy for engagement.

When two people get together too fast, the common advice is, "Slow down. Get to know each other." Yet few of us heed this counsel.

A man and I have been flirting for a year. We had 3 dates, then another man and I decided to be exclusive. But because the other man and I had struck up a good connection I asked if he'd like to remain friends.

We talk every two weeks and get together for coffee or a walk once a month. I always enjoy the conversations. He makes me laugh, is intellectually stimulating, emotionally stable, physically attractive, affectionate and brings qualities of character, ethics, and self-awareness I've not seen in others. When my then-beau and I broke up, I let this man know. We continued our regular talks, emails and get togethers, although it didn't escalate because he was between jobs and didn't have the bandwidth to take on a relationship, and I didn't really want to date a man who was unemployed.

The flirting has continued and in fact, escalated a bit. He sends loving and flirtatious emails and still calls every other week.

It feels like a low-speed chase.

I am used to men who are interested in me putting on a full-press pursuit pretty quickly. Although I've seen those fizzle after a few weeks or months. So this slower pace is foreign but appreciated. I don't feel like he's just trying to seduce me. I feel we're getting to know each other. It feels respectful.

Would I like the low-speed chase to quicken to a medium-speed chase? Yes and no. If he was employed, definitely. But while he's in this limbo I don't think it is wise to move to the next level.

Will I wait for him to get a job? I will continue to see other men and will welcome his contacts. He needs to decide he wants to step up the wooing, as I'm not going to pursue him. But I will keep sending him leads for jobs he's qualified for so I can help him get on his feet and hopefully increase his chase pace.

What do you think about slow- versus fast-paced chases? Which do you prefer?

Resources

Make sure to download your free eBook Attract Your Next Great Mate: Dating Advice From Top Relationship Experts *at www. DatingGoddess.com/freebie*

Afterword

At the time of this writing, I have not yet found my true King Charming. I continue my search with verve. I've become more discerning about what I want and don't want. I've met some wonderful men pals — my treasures — who continue to be in touch.

I wish you much luck in your adventure. It will be fun and frustrating, exhilarating and exasperating, and sexy or sexless. So much depends on you, your approach and your attitude. My books are designed to help you enjoy as much as possible and ward off unpleasantness. But nearly all adventures have wonderful highs as well as a few lows. If you know that going in and arm yourself with information on what to expect, you'll have more of the positives and fewer of the negatives.

Please drop by www.DatingGoddess.com and join in the discussion and report on your experiences.

Dating Goddess

Resources

Go to www.datinggoddess.com to access a variety of useful resources. We work to suggest resources we think have value.

Dating and relationship book reviews

These reviews will save you time and money as I've given you my take on specific books, CDs and more. Some are worth your effort to buy and read or listen to them — some are not. We're always adding new book reviews, so check frequently. We'll also notify our mailing list when new resources are added.

Dating site links

There are a lot of dating sites on the Internet. I've listed the ones I think are worth investigating.

Dating products and tools

Dating can be daunting. We're continually looking at

ways to make it easier and more fun. We'll provide info on games, tools, even date-wear that will help others know you're available, or help you get to know potential suitors better.

Dating and relationship advice sites

Advice "experts" abound on the Internet as anyone can self-proclaim themseves as expert — even if they haven't dated in 30 years and never in midlife. I've worked to find experts who's advice I generally think is solid.

Midlife recources

We'll feature Web sites, books, events and other resources we think might interest you.

Newly discovered resources

I'll add other resources as we discover them, subscribe to our mailing list to get the scoop as soon as we find them. Go to www.DatingGoddess.com to register for our mailing list. Don't worry, we won't sell or give your email to anyone.

Acknowledgments

Let me start by acknowledging the 112 men who helped trigger the lessons contained in this book. Some prompted several! They remain nameless here to protect their identity, although most would recognize references to them. Plus the thousands more whose winks, emails and calls didn't result in a date, but helped me learn the dating game. And all those men who I emailed who never responded — such a blessing to have them weed themselves out.

I acknowledge the 112 men who triggered my lessons

I'd like to thank my Seven Sisters mastermind group for the tremendous brainstorming, noodling, strategizing and encouragement. I wouldn't have begun this project without the prodding of Val Cade, Chris Clarke-Epstein, Mariah Burton Nelson, Sue Dyer, Sam Horn and Marilynn Mobley.

Thank you to my good friends who've listened to my dating stories ad nauseam, and whose support and wisdom are embedded in this text. Ed Betts, Ken Braly, Bruce Daley, Tom Drews, Elaine Floyd, Paulette Ensign, Scott Friedman, Craig Harrison, Mary Jansen, Tom Johnson, Sandy Jones, Mary Kilkenny, Ellie Klevins, Patrick Lynch, Mary Marcdante, Barbara McNichol, Ann Peterson, Anthony Ramsey, Caterina Rando, Kristy Rogers, Jana Stanfield, Holly Steil, Terry Tepliz, and George Walther, thank you.

The Adventures in Delicious Dating After 40 series

The *Adventures in Delicious Dating After 40* series is designed to help you understand your own midlife dating journey. It is not a road map, as we all take different routes. It is a guide to help you understand yourself, midlife men, and the dating process. Hopefully, you'll not only learn from the lessons and insights shared in this series, but you'll examine how they apply — or don't — to your own dating adventure.

You'll get the scoop on what you need to know, what's changed since you last dated, and how to navigate inevitable bumps in the road.

Following is an overview of each book in the series and a sampling of some of the chapter titles. All are detailed at www.DatingGoddess.com.

Date or Wait: Are You Ready for Mr. Great?

Are you ready for a special man in your life? You have a great life. But you know you'd like a special man to share it. You think you're ready to date, but you haven't done it in a while.

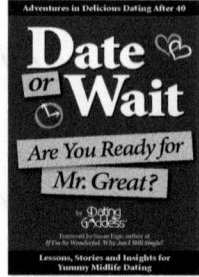

What should you consider before you actually start dating full bore? Even if you've reentered the dating world, this will give you a foundation of attitude and philosophy to make your adventure more fulfilling.

Sample chapters

♥ From hurt to flirt

♥ Dating is like Baskin-Robbins

♥ You've got to kiss a lot of…princes!

♥ What's your definition of dating success?

♥ Are you open to receiving?

♥ Dating: A self-designed personal-growth workshop

♥ Hands-on dating research

♥ Being present to the presents

♥ Being aggressively single

♥ Approaching dating like a buffet

♥ Is Brad Pitt ruining your love life?

♥ Treasures can come in dented packages

Assessing Your Assets: Why You're A Great Catch

You have many wonderful qualities. But it's easy to focus on one's flaws — at least what seem like flaws to you. However, to the right man your imperfections are endearing, attractive and lovable. You have to be clear what you offer a man who will find you enchanting.

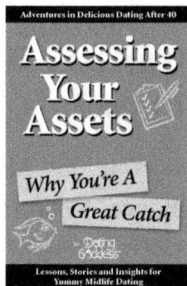

Assessing Your Assets helps you look at what you bring to a new relationship. It will help you see your good points so you'll approach dating with more confidence.

Sample chapters

❤ Don't think you are damaged goods

❤ You are (probably) more attractive than you think!

❤ They aren't called "hate handles"

❤ Are you a good man picker?

❤ What are your deal breakers?

❤ Are you arguing your limitations?

❤ Turn your liabilities into assets

❤ The strong vs. nice woman debate

❤ Is your sense of humor stunting your dating?

❤ Why are we drawn to bad boys?

❤ The zest test

In Search of King Charming: Who Do I Want to Share My Throne?

You are no longer looking for "Prince" Charming because you are a queen. You want someone who is at your level, not groveling at your feet. You want a king — someone who's your equal and with whom you can rule the throne together!

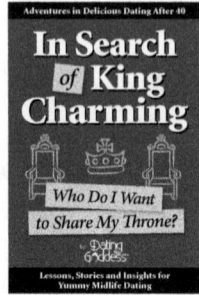

This book focuses on helping you better define what you want beyond tall, dark and handsome! You'll consider characteristics you might not have thought of before. You'll look at what you want now.

Sample chapters

💜 Building your Franken-boyfriend

💜 What's your "perfect boyfriend's" job description?

💜 A man to go with your wardrobe

💜 In search of the elusive good kisser

💜 When you're clear on what you want, it appears

💜 Are you dating the same guy in different bodies?

💜 Does he fit in your world?

💜 What's your kissing quotient?

💜 Is your guy's loving muscle strong?

💜 Do you both have the same dating rhythm?

Embracing Midlife Men:
Insights Into Curious Behaviors

Do you sometimes scratch your head after interacting with a midlife man, wondering, "What could he possibly be thinking?" Especially if it's before, during or after a date with a man who presumably wants to impress you!

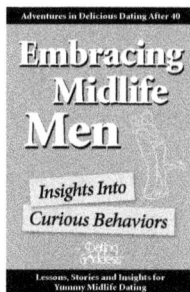

This book focuses on better understanding midlife men's behaviors. When you grasp what's going on in his head it's much easier to embrace him. Men are wondrous creatures, so we need to understand them better and love them for who they are.

Sample chapters

💜 Men are like shoes

💜 Why men disappear when it gets serious

💜 Chivalry isn't dead —but it seems to be hibernating

💜 Do men want feisty women?

💜 Midlife men have forgotten how to date

💜 Are you getting prime time from your man?

💜 When a man tells you what he paid for things

💜 Does he treat you like his ex?

💜 Has Greg Behrendt done women a disservice?

💜 Tales of woo

Dipping Your Toe in the Dating Pool: Dive In Without Belly Flopping

You've decided you are ready — you want to start dating. Maybe you've already had a few coffee dates with several men. You want to be as successful as possible on your dating adventure.

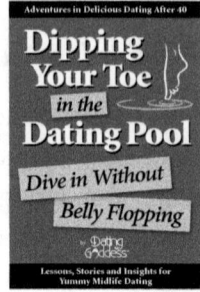

This book focuses on getting started on your dating adventures. We cover what you need to know as you begin your journey.

Sample chapters

💜 Do you have the right datewear?

💜 Dating with integrity

💜 Building your rejection muscle

💜 When "be yourself" is questionable advice

💜 Faux beaus and practice dating

💜 Are you making bad decisions out of loneliness?

💜 Being "in wonder" about your date's behavior

💜 When do you feel most vulnerable in dating?

💜 Are you out of his league — or he yours?

💜 Why listening is so seductive

Winning at the Online Dating Game: Stack the Deck in Your Favor

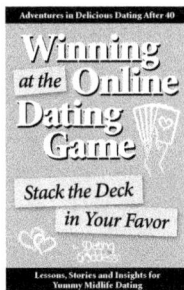

Internet dating can be frustrating or fruitful. It will be much less exasperating if you know how to read and weed out men's profiles that aren't appropriate for you. And you'll have a steady stream of potential suitors if you know how to write a compelling profile for yourself.

This book focuses on the ins and outs of online dating. How to play the game, which has it's own rules and language. If you don't understand how online dating works, you'll waste a lot of time connecting with men who are not a possible fit for you.

Sample chapters

💚 Shopping for men

💚 Safe online dating

💚 Is 21st Century dating unnatural?

💚 What do men look at in your profile?

💚 Euphemisms uncovered

💚 Are you describing yourself compellingly?

💚 No, I will not be dating your Harley

💚 Playing the online dating game

💚 Scantily clothed pictures

Check Him Out Before Going Out: Avoiding Dud Dates

Under the cloak of the anonymity that email and the phone provides, men often reveal more than they intend. If you ask the right questions you can find out a lot about his values and view of the world after just an interaction or two.

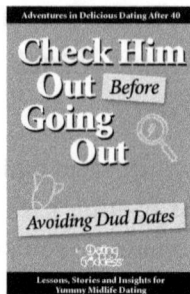

This book focuses on what you need to ask before agreeing to even a coffee date. You need to vet the men who email and call you to ensure you're not likely to waste your time with men who clearly aren't a match.

Sample chapters

❤ Becoming smitten with the fantasy

❤ Can Google help — or hinder — your dating life?

❤ Qualify your potential dates before meeting

❤ The art of consideration

❤ Anticipating a big date is like awaiting Santa

❤ Being seduced by what he is over who he is

❤ Are you his spare?

❤ My boyfriend, whom I haven't met

❤ When canceling is the right thing to do

❤ Politics, religion and sex — oh my!

First-Rate First Dates: Increasing the Chances of a Second Date

You can tell a lot about someone within the first 30 minutes. What does he talk about? Does he ask you questions? If so, what does he want to know about you? What do you need to know about him? How does he treat you? How does he treat those around you?

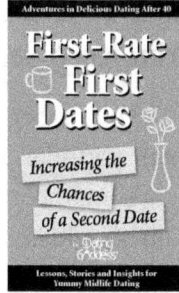

This book focuses on what goes on during the first date. How do you determine if you want a second date? What you can do to increase the likelihood your date will ask you for a second? That is if you want a repeat!

Sample chapters

💜 Start with coffee

💜 How do you greet him?

💜 When it clicks, throw out some of your criteria

💜 Tracking your date's score

💜 Clues a guy is just looking for a booty call

💜 12 signs he won't be asking for a second date

💜 First-date red flags that this guy isn't for you

💜 Honesty is not always the best policy

💜 Chemistry, or does he make my toes curl?

💜 Women's first-date blunders

Real Deal or Faux Beau: Should You Keep Seeing Him?

You've begun to go out with a man you like. How do you decide if you should continue seeing him, or if you should release him because he's not The One?

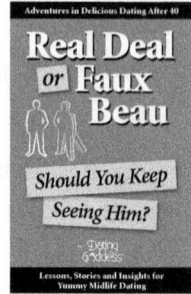

This book focuses on second dates and beyond. During the dating process you are both assessing if you want to keep seeing each other. This book helps you determine what questions you need to ask yourself.

Sample chapters

💜 Deciding to see him again or not

💜 What's your date's Delight/Disappointment Scale score?

💜 Broaching tough conversations

💜 "I want to respect me in the morning"

💜 Does he invite you to his place?

💜 Are you stingy in dating?

💜 When his hand is on your knee too soon

💜 Easy way to ask hard questions

💜 Rose-colored glasses obscure red flags

💜 If his stories don't add up, subtract yourself

Multidating Responsibly: Play the Field Without Being A Player

Playing the field is frowned on in some circles. There are definitely appropriate and inappropriate ways to date several men simultaneously.

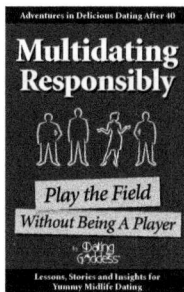

Adventures in Delicious Dating After 40

Multidating Responsibly

Play the Field
Without Being A Player

by Dating Goddess

Lessons, Stories and Insights for Yummy Midlife Dating

This book focuses on how to date around responsibly and with integrity without leading men on. If you do it with honesty, you can date several people at once until you're both ready to focus only on each other.

Sample chapters

💚 "Pimpin'" — Dating multiple guys

💚 Multi-dating pros and cons

💚 Your Date-A-Base — tracking multiple suitors

💚 "Hot bunking" your beaus

💚 Are you a "Let's Make a Deal" type of dater?

💚 Assume there are other women

💚 Dating's revolving door

💚 How long do you hedge your bet?

💚 Beware of multi-tasking when multi-dating

💚 Back burner beaus

💚 The boyfriend phone

Moving On Gracefully: Break Up Without Heartache

"Breaking up" sounds so high school, doesn't it? But part of the dating process is saying something when one of you decides not to date the other anymore. Going "poof" is not a mature or respectful option in midlife.

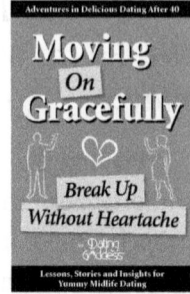

This book focuses on surviving a breakup, whether you initiate it or not. Either way, it's never easy to break up if you have developed any fondness toward the other.

Sample chapters

🖤 Hello — goodbye: How to say no thanks after meeting

🖤 Releasing back into the dating pool

🖤 50 ways to leave your lover? 4 ways not to leave your suitor

🖤 Breaking up is hard to do — right

🖤 Why men go "poof"

🖤 How to trump being dumped

🖤 When breaking up is a "Get Out of Jail Free" card

🖤 How to detect the end is near

🖤 Failed relationships' blessings

🖤 He's broken up with you — he just didn't tell you

🖤 Rejection is protection

From Fear to Frolic: Get Naked Without Getting Embarrassed

This book focuses on what you need to consider and know before getting physically intimate with a man you're dating. This is nerve-wracking to many midlife women. This book will prepare you.

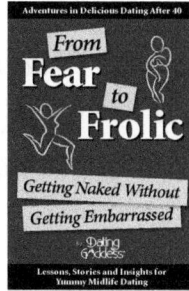

Sample chapters

💜 Sleepover do's and don'ts

💜 Does he want in your life — or just in your bedroom?

💜 Getting naked with him the first time

💜 An excuse to seduce or how important is bedroom bliss?

💜 What to ask yourself before getting naked with him

💜 Are you and your guy on the same sexual time line?

💜 Sharing your sexual owner's manual with him

💜 What women need from a man before having sex

💜 Why too-soon midlife sex is like non-fat food

💜 How dating sex is like waffles

💜 Too-soon seduction: "I'm special, but not THAT special"

Ironing Out Dating Wrinkles: Work Through Challenges Without Getting Steamed

Nearly all relationships have some ups and downs. Part of getting to know someone is knowing how they work through relationship misunderstandings.

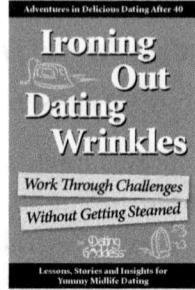

This book focuses on how to work through the inevitable hiccups that happen when you are getting to know each other. If you can both deal with challenges, the bond deepens and you find yourself smitten.

Sample chapters

🖤 When your guy vexes you, ask what your highest self would do

🖤 The first fight

🖤 You want boo; he wants boo-ty

🖤 Where's the line between getting your needs met and being selfish?

🖤 Expressing your upset with your guy

🖤 Is his toothbrush in your cabinet too soon?

🖤 Do you love how he loves you?

🖤 Is he collecting data on how to make you happy?

🖤 Be careful of being smitten

🖤 Exclusivity: How and when to broach it